WHAT TO EXPECT
FROM THE
HOLY SPIRIT

WHAT TO EXPECT
FROM THE
HOLY SPIRIT

Dr. Earl D. Radmacher

WHAT TO EXPECT FROM THE HOLY SPIRIT
© 2014 by Dr. Earl D. Radmacher

Published by Redeeming Press
Dallas, OR 97338
RedeemingPress.com

This book was originally published by Radio Bible Class in 1983.

ISBN: 978-1-939992-31-4 (Paperback)
ISBN: 978-1-939992-32-1 (Mobi)
ISBN: 978-1-939992-33-8 (ePub)

All rights reserved. No part of this publication may be reproduced, stored in or introduced into a retrieval system, or transmitted, in any form, or by any means—electronic, mechanical, photocopying, recording, or otherwise—except for brief quotations, without the prior written permission of both the copyright owner and the publisher of this book.

Unless otherwise indicated, all Scripture quotations are taken from the New American Standard Bible. ©The Lockman Foundation 1960, 1962, 1963, 1968, 1971, 1972, 1973, 1975, 1977. Used by permission. All rights reserved.

Scripture quotations marked "NIV" are from The Holy Bible, New International Version®, NIV® Copyright © 1973, 1978, 1984, 2011 by Biblica, Inc.® Used by permission. All rights reserved worldwide.

Cover Image by Pozitiw / 123RF Stock Photo
Cover Design by Jeremy Myers

TABLE OF CONTENTS

Tribute 7
Publisher's Preface 9
Foreword 13

Introduction 17
The Pattern of Dependence 23
The Power for Witness 35
The Protector of the Church 51
The Provider of the Gifts 67
The Possessor of the Body Member 81
Conclusion 97

Appendix 101
About the Author 113

TRIBUTE

The following letter was written by Dr. Chuck Swindoll to Dr. Earl Radmacher on October 2003 in honor of Dr. Radmacher's lifetime of ministry, scholarship, and service.

My memory of Earl Radmacher takes me back to the fall of 1959 through the spring of 1962, when Earl and Ruth lived in a little apartment only a stone's throw from Campus Apartments, where Cynthia and I spent our four years at Dallas Theological Seminary. Earl was in his mid-to-late twenties, working on his doctorate at the time and also teaching theology as Dr. John Walvoord's assistant. So, I got to know Earl up close and personal, not only as a fellow student but also as a faculty member. What great memories I have of his fine, exuberant, strong-hearted, clean shaven (!) young man! The word was out around our campus back then—"Watch this guy; he's going somewhere!"

And he certainly has!

What to Expect from the Holy Spirit

It's been a joy to watch the Lord use my friend during these years in various capacities, all of them significant. I have always known that wherever he served, he was standing strong in the Lord, firmly committed to the truths of God's inerrant Word, and faithfully devoted to his wife and their children. Only one problem that I can think of when it comes to Earl—you never really know what he believes, since he's so reluctant to speak out and he so seldom makes waves. You're laughing … so am I! On the contrary, in a culture that is now willing to tolerate anything and embrace all things, it is refreshing to know there are still a few prophet-like souls who aren't afraid to stand up, speak out, and say it straight when it comes to the main things.

Hat's off to you, Dr. Earl Radmacher—I love you and I respect you. It delights me to know that you are being honored today, which is only a taste of the many rewards awaiting you as you kneel before our glorious Lord Jesus Christ and hear His, "Well done, good and faithful servant."

With loud applause for your life and ministry,

Chuck Swindoll
October 16, 2003

PUBLISHER'S PREFACE

What to Expect from the Holy Spirit was originally published by RBC Ministries in 1983 and helped countless numbers of people understand the ministry and work of the Holy Spirit in their lives as followers of Jesus. I thank RBC Ministries for allowing Redeeming Press to get this book back into print.

I trust the updated and revised edition of this essential study will encourage people to understand the role of the Spirit in helping them conform into the image and likeness of Jesus Christ, spread the Gospel around the world, and clarify some of the confusion that often accompanies teaching about Spiritual gifts and the filling of the Holy Spirit.

The original 1983 edition of this book consisted of the transcriptions of several messages that Dr. Earl Radmacher had given on the topic of the Holy Spirit at Moody Bible Institute's "Founder's Week" in 1980, and which were then aired on the radio by Radio Bible Class. As such, some of the terminology and language used in the original edition of this book were specifically geared toward a listening audience. For example, the book contained numerous invitations for the audience to turn to a certain passage in their Bibles and statements by Dr. Radmacher about him looking down at the text. While such phraseology is good preaching and teaching technique, it somewhat hinders the thought flow for any person reading the text. So in this edition, I have tried to remove or reword many of these sorts of comments so that the original transcriptions read more like a book.

A few other minor changes were made to the text as well, such as removing a few statements about the "future" decade of the 1980's and correcting a few Bible references so that they are used consistently throughout. No changes were made whatsoever to any of Dr. Radmacher's ideas or theology about the Holy Spirit.

On a more personal note, I am particularly thrilled to be able to get this book back into print because it is precisely many of the truths contained within this book which helped me gain a proper perspective on the Holy Spirit in my early days as a young pastor. I was 25 years old and in my first church when Dr. Radmacher graciously agreed to come speak in the church I pastored. Like most churches, we had our fair share of struggles and disagreements about the ministry and role of the Holy Spirit in our church service, and I remember being amazed at how Dr. Radmacher taught us about the Holy Spirit with clarity, authority, and most of all, grace.

What struck me most as a young pastor was when Dr. Radmacher taught about how the Holy Spirit was

Publisher's Preface

not interested in starting a Holy Spirit movement, but was only interested in exalting the name of Jesus, in lifting His name up, and in drawing all people to Him. Dr. Radmacher said then (as he says in this book), "The Spirit of God has only the desire to focus on Jesus Christ." Church pastors and ministry leaders may sound spiritual when they spend all their time talking about the Holy Spirit, but if they were *really* filled with the Holy Spirit, He would lead them to focus their lives, their ministries, and their teachings on Jesus. In my decades of ministry since that time, I have endeavored to follow the advice of Dr. Radmacher—and the leading of the Holy Spirit—in this regard. With the Apostle Paul, I have sought to know nothing but Christ, and Him crucified. As you read this book, I think you will be encouraged to do the same.

So thank you for reading. I trust that as you read, your life, your mind, and your spirit will be blessed as the truth about the Holy Spirit is unfolded to you by one of the best and most influential Bible scholars and of the past 100 years.

Jeremy Myers
June 2014

Foreword

By Dr. Stephen R. Lewis
President, Rocky Mountain Bible College & Seminary

[Publisher's Note: This Foreword was not in the original edition of this book, but has been added to introduce what Dr. Earl Radmacher writes about the Holy Spirit on the following pages.]

What was true of the sixties, seventies, and even the eighties remains true today. We too live in a time that can be described with words like "revolution," "fighting," "apathy," and "lethargy." But today, these terms can also describe the church, especially in relation to the Holy Spirit. While the sixties did bring a renewed awareness of the person and work of the Holy Spirit, the church "backed into" the current focus of the Holy Spirit.

Throughout the history of the church, most clarifications of doctrine have come as a reaction against some teaching. Within the first three centuries following the Apostles, theological errors arose, not from evil intentions of church leaders, but from their desire to find answers to everyday pastoral questions and to help people understand the text. Yet instead of going back to the biblical text (as it existed at that time) to form their theological views, they often turned to the writings of previous generations. Gradually, the vagueness of the early Christian (post New Testament) writings gave way to error. As the use of the Bible faded out, theology—developed by consensus at Church Councils—became increasingly dogmatic and philosophical.[1] By the time of the invention of the printing press, theology—deeply rooted in philosophy—was already "complete." All the questions had been asked and answered. Orthodoxy had been defined and little room was left for studies of the original text. Theologians focused their studies on the works of someone else who studied the works of someone else who studied the works of

---

[1] Vincent of Lerins (5th Century AD), for instance, "[had] long been engaged in what we today call an empirical inquiry, a careful sampling process, something like a poll-taking exercise. He was deliberately inquiring of many believers, especially those well-grounded in sanctity, asking this simple question: How does the whole church come to distinguish the truth of Christian faith from falsehood amid conflicted opinions? ... Again the answer rings clear from all he asks—an answer that has become known as the Vincentian rule: In the world-wide community of believers every care should be taken to hold fast to what has been believed everywhere, always and by all." See Thomas C. Oden, *The Rebirth of Orthodoxy: Signs of New Life in Christianity* (New York, HarperCollins Publishers: 2003), 161-162. My take is that the councils represent only a partial-consensus. Group A forms a consensus that Group B is wrong. For example, Eastern Orthodox (Greek) claim a different consensus than those who are not.

Foreword

someone else (and so on) and to debate the opinions expressed by their predecessors.[2]

Yet it has occasionally seemed that something was lacking. That something was missing. That some changed was required or some deficiency needed to be corrected in the answers provided by our predecessors.

Many in recent decades have suggested that one deficiency in the theology of our forebears was in the area of Pneumatology—the study of the Holy Spirit. Yet as many in Christianity have sought to fill this void, they have sometimes turned to personal experience as their primary instructor, or worse yet, have turned to the spiritual writings of other religions for help in understanding the spiritual realm.

This book by Dr. Earl Radmacher attempts to answer the question of the Holy Spirit differently. This book seeks to determine from the Scriptures what we can know about the person and work of the Holy Spirit in our lives today.

Furthermore this book makes the important case that the particular work of the Holy Spirit is to serve as a witness to Jesus Christ, not just to who He is and what He has done, but also to what He offers to the world. This means that as we go forward in the power of the Holy Spirit, we will serve as Spirit-filled witnesses to the world concerning their need for the free gift of everlasting life, which is by grace alone, through faith alone, in Jesus Christ alone, to the glory of God alone!

---

[2] There were occasional innovators who worked with portions of the text (e.g., Luther worked in Romans), but their students had a strong tendency to study the innovators' work rather than follow the example in studying the Word.

Yet the work of the Spirit does not stop there. Dr. Radmacher points out that believers are to be aware of the work of the Holy Spirit in empowering church leaders to equip the church to do the work of ministry (see Ephesians 4:11-13 where the Apostles and Prophets are a part of the foundation that has already been laid). When believers submit to those in authority over them, they are being "… diligent to preserve the unity of the Spirit in the bond of peace" (Ephesians 4:3-6).

Finally, if there is one thing that is missing among conservative, evangelical, Bible-believing, Gospel-living Christians, it is the lack of discovering and implementing their spiritual gifts. So often, when I have taught on the subject of spiritual gifts, I have asked the congregation "How many here believe God has given at least one spiritual gift to every believer?" They have almost always all responded by the raising of their hands. Later, if I asked them, "How many believe God, through the Holy Spirit, has given each of *you* at least one spiritual gift?" only a handful responds positively. This is the problem: Few of us have learned "What to expect from the Holy Spirit." This book will point you in the right direction.

INTRODUCTION

I recently asked people in various groups for one-word descriptions of the sixties. The responses that came back were words like "riot," "rebellion," "revolution," and "fighting." Then I asked them about the seventies, and they used terms like "apathy," "indifference," "indolence," and "lethargy." Notice the similarity in the words various people used to describe those decades. The same sort of pattern would probably be found if people were asked to provide words for more recent decades as well.

So often we see only one perspective. Though the 1960's are often thought of as a time of fighting and rebellion, some beautiful things happened along with the ugly things. One of the beautiful things that happened in the sixties was the renewed enthusiasm for and study of the subject of spiritual gifts. Before 1960, you would have been hard pressed to find one book in print on the full doctrine of spiritual gifts as taught in the Word of God. You may have found books on one of the individual gifts, but no book on the biblical doctrine of all the spiritual gifts was available. The subject simply was not talked about in mainline evangelicalism.

When such a glaring omission happens in history, God may even use man's errors to precipitate a renewed study of the neglected doctrine. In effect, He drives us back into the Word of God to find out what the truth is. In my estimation, the men who began talking about the gifts of the Spirit in the sixties presented teaching that contained error. Nonetheless, they got Bible scholars started, and that eventually led to a flood of books on spiritual gifts, and there is probably still room for more good books on this vital topic.

Through the riot and revolution of the sixties, the people were crying out for identity. They were wanting to be heard. But their plea had a selfish, humanistic thrust. In the midst of the world's clamor for identity, God's people were given the opportunity to see His means of receiving identity. Paul the apostle stated it clearly in Romans 12:3, a neglected verse:

> *For through the grace given to me I say to every man among you not to think more highly of himself than he ought to think; but to think so as to have sound judgment, as God has allotted to each a measure of faith.*
> *~Romans 12:3*

Before I can contribute to the unity of the church or the unity of the family, I must understand my own identity. I will never be able to contribute effectively to unity until I first understand who I am. Identity! In the sixties, God brought that idea to the fore, and more has

Introduction

been said on that subject since 1960 than had been said from the time of the first-century church up to that day.

In the seventies, God did another marvelous thing. This decade was called the "narcissistic age," the "me generation," the "self-centered society." But it was also the first time that I recall a book on God becoming a bestseller. Before the seventies, you could have counted on one hand the books in print written about God that were worth the time to read.

One of those books was *The Knowledge of the Holy*, authored by the great Bible scholar and pulpiteer A. W. Tozer. Did you know that Tozer apologized for writing that book? He felt that it was not worthy of the subject matter. But he said, "Before I die, I must write something on God. Somebody has to write something on God. Everything we hear and read," he added, "is about man and what man is like." Tozer was one of the first in modern times to get excited about the study of God.

Then there was a man from England (Trinity College, Bristol), James I. Packer, who had written a few little magazine articles on a big subject: God. He never dreamed that they would be put together in a book; even less did he dream that the book from those articles, *Knowing God*, would become a bestseller! Further, it would open the way for a plethora of books on the person, the attributes, and the excellencies of God since that time.

How ironic that in the decade called the "narcissistic age," the "me generation," the "self-centered society," we had an explosion of great materials on what God is like!

I believe that our growing understanding of the God of the gifts coupled with our growing knowledge and implementation of those gifts can give us the resources we need to move into a tremendous harvest in the coming decades. I believe that America has the potential of being either wiped out or having a greater revival than it has seen since the Great Awakening. And I believe that much of it will have to do with our response to the way God has brought our attention to Himself. It will depend upon what we do with who He is, who we are, and how we put those two truths together to meet the magnificent opportunity before us.

I personally believe that the coming decades are going to be the most challenging and exciting times I have ever seen. I look forward to them with keen anticipation. I am expecting good things because the darker the night becomes, the brighter the light shines.

I am glad we are done (it is hoped) with "the good life." The opportunity of the church is best in times of famine, persecution, and trouble. Now, I want to assure you I am not praying for that. I am too chicken-hearted for that. I would like to believe that it is somehow possible for us to experience revival short of persecution. I do not have historical precedent for it, but I still pray that a great spiritual awakening will occur. Eighty-five percent of the money and resources controlled by Christians in the world is controlled by Christians in America. And if somehow we will quit sitting on it and begin investing it—not in things but in people who make a difference—I believe we will see another great awakening.

Introduction

In Jonathan Edwards' day, preachers focused on the study of what God is like, and they preached about what God is like. Whenever people have given their attention to the study of God, things have changed. I am told that in a town of approximately 1,000 people, 900 were eventually drawn to Jonathan Edwards' church—because he preached on the character of God. He was not necessarily a man with a lot of charisma. As I understand it, he was a rather tall and spare fellow who leaned over the pulpit and, of all things, read his manuscript in a monotone voice to the people. And history records that the audible distress and weeping of the people for fear that they would drop off into the "dreadful furnace" of hell before he finished his message obliged Edwards to request silence so that he might be heard.

I pray that God will give me an increasing appreciation of what He is like. The world says that the proper study for man is *man*. But if that is your object, you will never rise any higher than yourself. The proper study for man is not *man*; the proper study for man is *God*. It is altogether fitting that the creature should study the Creator if he is to rise any higher than his present level. No man will ever walk any higher in Christ than His knowledge of God. You cannot live higher than your understanding of what He is like. If you have a weak, anemic concept of God, you cannot help but have a weak, anemic faith and consequently a weak, anemic life.

Right action begins with right thinking, and right thinking begins with thinking right about what God is like. That is why the wise king who wrote Proverbs said, "The fear of the Lord is the beginning of knowledge" (Proverbs 1:7). And the psalmist wrote, "The fear of the Lord is the beginning of wisdom" (Psalm 111:10). This is having due respect for who God is and what He is really like. Little wonder that Jesus said in His prayer, "This is eternal life, that they may know Thee, the only true God, and Jesus Christ whom Thou hast sent" (John 17:3).

"That they may know Thee." Every time I read that statement, I am convicted of how often someone has said to me, "When did you come to know Christ?" I say, "Oh, when I was 14 years of age at Twin Rocks Boys Camp." All of a sudden I go back to this verse. Knowing God is not something that happened to me in a split second of time. I came into the family of God in an instant; however, knowing God is a lifetime of coming to understand Him, and it will go on for all eternity. The author of Hebrews said, "Let us draw near with a sincere heart in full assurance of faith" (Hebrews 10:22). Draw near to whom? Draw near to God! Daniel stated the same truth when he said, "… the people who know their God will display strength and take action" (Daniel 11:32).

As we learn more of God, and more particularly one person of the Godhead, the Holy Spirit, let us heed the exhortation of Ephesians 5:1, "Therefore, be imitators of God." To mimic somebody is not considered to be a good art form. The emphasis today is on originality. But in Paul's day it was the best art form. It was an attempt to duplicate, as exactly as possible, another. Thus Paul did not hesitate to tell us to imitate himself and also Christ. "Therefore, be imitators of God."

1

THE PATTERN OF DEPENDENCE

In this first chapter on the subject of God the Holy Spirit and His pattern of living for the believer, I would like to ask several questions. The first is foundational. What can we imitate in God? I believe certain *attributes* and *actions* of God can be imitated by believers.

ATTRIBUTES TO BE IMITATED

Obviously, we cannot imitate the infinity, the eternity, nor the immutability of God. But according to Scripture, we can imitate His holiness (Leviticus 11:44).

I believe that if there is a central attribute of God, then holiness is that central attribute. I cannot accept the statement that love is the central attribute of God—even a proper form of love. (I do not think our generation basically understands love, because it has interpreted it as sentimentality or warm feelings. That is much different from biblical love.) Love is a "how"; holiness is a "what." Before you can do the "how," you have to know the "what." Before you can love, you have to know what the standard of love is. And that standard is holiness.

This distinction is clearly seen in Paul's letter to the church at Philippi. The people of this congregation were rich in love and warm experience, but their love was in danger of distortion because they had failed to root it in knowledge. Thus Paul prayed these words:

> *"... that your love may abound still more and more in real knowledge and all discernment, so that you may approve the things that are excellent, in order to be sincere and blameless until the day of Christ."*
> *~Philippians 1:9-10*

In other words, love that is not according to knowledge will find itself approving things that are not excellent. Therefore, love needs to be controlled by an understanding of God's standard of holiness.

A parallel in the physical world may be seen in water or fire. Water confined within boundaries of control is useful and productive, such as the water used in irrigation. But water in a flood, monsoon, or hurricane is destructive. Likewise, fire contained within the chambers of a blast furnace is productive; however, fire sweeping through a forest is destructive. So it is with love. Love that is controlled by holiness is productive; love uncontrolled by such a standard is destructive.

The Pattern of Dependence

There can be no real love, therefore, apart from an understanding of holiness.

A graphic example of what happens when love and holiness are separated is seen in the application of situation ethics, a viewpoint designated as the "new morality" in the mid-1950s by its architect, Joseph Fletcher. Situational ethics declares that there are no absolutes except love. Laws, rules, and commandments are all set aside. Thus Fletcher rewrote the Ten Commandments as follows: "Thou shalt not kill—ordinarily"; "Thou shalt not commit adultery—ordinarily." To him, killing, adultery, or other sins would be right and proper if they were given a loving motive and situation. In other words, he applied the maxim "The end justifies the means" to morality.

Is it any wonder, then, that people today are having great difficulty discerning between right and wrong? For example, our society made a decision about abortion that has resulted in the murder of millions of infants over the last several decades. As might have been expected, a further step was then suggested; namely, a probationary period *after birth* to determine whether a baby's defects are such that its life should be ended. The logic is as follows: abortion prior to birth is sometimes based on a question mark because the parents did not know with certainty whether or not the child would be born permanently disabled. But within a short period of time after birth, the severity of the defect can be known and the reason for termination of life made certain.

If this kind of logic seems scary, then remember— it's the natural result of a value-system that is not based on God's holy law. It is not unlike the thinking of Hitler's Germany, which reasoned that it was appropriate to sterilize men and women considered biologically unfit to propagate the species, or to exterminate those who were considered no longer useful in building the master race.

ACTIONS TO BE IMITATED

Not only are there *attributes* of God that we can imitate, but we are to imitate certain of His *actions* as well. Not His act of creation, of course. We are incapable of generating something out of nothing. But one of the specific acts of God we would do well to imitate today is that of dependency or submission.

You are undoubtedly asking, how does God demonstrate dependency? In developing the doctrine of the triune God from Scripture, theologians speak of the *ontological trinity* and the *economic trinity*. In referring to the ontological trinity, the trinity of being, we understand that God the Father, the Son, and the Holy Spirit are, for example, coequal and coeternal. Each person of the trinity possesses all of the attributes of God. In being, one person of the trinity is not inferior to another.

We also recognize that God has revealed Himself in a work relationship. We refer to that as the economic trinity. In that work relationship, the sovereign God, who cannot display dependency to anyone or anything outside of Himself, displays dependency within Himself. Therefore, in the economy of the trinity—within the Godhead—there is an example for me of dependency. God the Father is the architect (so to speak) of the plan of redemption. God the Son, in submission to God the Father, carried out the plan and paid the price of man's redemption. God the Holy Spirit, in submission to the Father and the Son, carries out their directions in applying that redemption.

God also demonstrated to us in His Word, both by precept and by practice, the principle of dependency or submission. Think of the passage, for example, in 1 Corinthians 11 where Paul was about to enter into a practical situation with regard to the role of men and women in the church. He wrote:

Be imitators of me, just as I also am of Christ.

Now I praise you because you remember me in everything, and hold firmly to the traditions, just as I delivered them to you.

But I want you to understand that Christ is the head of every man, and the man is the head of a woman, and God is the head of Christ.
- 1 Corinthians 11:1-3

Jesus Christ is headed by God the Father. Jesus Christ, who is coequal and coeternal with the Father, is nonetheless in submission to the Father. Consider the beautiful prayer of Christ to the Father in John 17. Every line breathes submission. You could not find a greater demonstration in Scripture. God is the head of Christ. Christ submitted to the Father.

The same truth of submission was taught by Christ throughout the upper room discourse, especially when it related to the Holy Spirit. Whereas Jesus is said to be sent by the Father (John 14:24; 17:3, 8, 21, 23, 25), the Holy Spirit is said to be sent by both the Father and the Son.

Let me note two specific verses:

But the Helper, the Holy Spirit, whom the Father will send in My name, He will teach you all things, and bring to your remembrance all that I said to you (John 14:26).

When the Helper comes, whom I will send to you from the Father, that is the Spirit of truth, who proceeds from the Father, He will bear witness of Me.
~John 15:26

It would not be the work of the Holy Spirit to initiate nor to create. His work would be to bring to the disciples' remembrance the things that Christ had taught them. In submission to the Son of God, the Spirit of God had the work of illuminating that which the Son had said. It was not the Spirit's job to speak of Himself; it was the Spirit's job to speak of Christ. Read these important words of Christ:

But when He, the Spirit of truth, comes, He will guide you into all the truth; for He will not speak on His own initiative, but whatever He hears, He will speak; and He will disclose to you what is to come.

> *He shall glorify Me; for He shall take of Mine, and shall disclose it to you.*
>
> *All things that the Father has are Mine; therefore I said, that He takes of Mine, and will disclose it to you.*
>
> *~John 16:13-15*

If God the Holy Spirit could take that position of submission, how much easier it should be for me, not having His credentials, to imitate that pattern of submission.

THE PRACTICAL APPLICATION

Finally, how can you and I imitate in practicality the pattern of the Holy Spirit in dependence? This question is answered in 1 Corinthians 12. In speaking to the Corinthian church, Paul was confronting one of the most carnal, rebellious, self-centered, divisive churches of the first century. They considered themselves very spiritual; in fact, they were not lacking in any spiritual gift. They were eagerly awaiting the coming of the Lord (1 Corinthians 1:7). Yet they were not about to be in submission to anybody—let alone Paul (1 Corinthians 4:6-14). The apostle handled them with a little more feistiness, I guess, than some of the other churches when he said:

> *Now concerning spiritual gifts, brethren, I do not want you to be unaware. You know that when you*

> *were pagans, you were led astray to the dumb idols, however you were led.*
>
> *Therefore I make known to you, that non one speaking by the Spirit of God says, "Jesus is accursed;" and no one can say, "Jesus is Lord," except by the Holy Spirit.*
>
> *~ 1 Corinthians 12:1-3*

What does it mean for a person to say "Jesus is accursed," or "Jesus is Lord"? Obviously, in this passage the apostle was not talking about the mere utterance of the word, but of the principle behind them. Suppose I go down to a tavern and offer a drunken man five dollars if he will say "Jesus is Lord." I guarantee you that he will say "Jesus is Lord" in order to get the five dollars! In such a case, is this man speaking by the Holy Spirit? No, Paul was not talking about meaningless, empty slogans. He was saying that no one can own Jesus as Lord except by the Holy Spirit. In like fashion, no one who is speaking by the Holy Spirit will ever demean Jesus.

How does that work out in faith and practice? Let me give you a possibility. Someone comes along and says, "Have you received the Spirit?" You say, "Yes, I was born again back in August of 1962 and the Spirit of God took up residence in me. My body became His temple" (see 1 Corinthians 6:19). Then he says, "Oh, yes, I know that; but I mean more than that. Since then, have you spoken in tongues and been baptized in the Spirit?"

The Pattern of Dependence

When someone says this to me, I challenge them with 1 Corinthians 12:3, because he is implying that there is something more to be received than that which I was given when I believed in Jesus Christ—and to do that is to demean Christ. No man who is speaking by the Spirit of God will ever pull Jesus away from center stage. God put Jesus in the spotlight. He is to have the preeminence (Colossians 1:18, 19). He is the Head of the church. The focus is to be on Jesus, and the Spirit of God does exactly that. Christ said, "He shall glorify Me" (John 16:14).

If I want to imitate the Godhead in the pattern of dependency, what will I do? I will throw the focus of attention on Jesus Christ and honor Him just as the Spirit of God does.

This came home to me vividly several years ago. I was in Melbourne, Australia, presenting a series on the spiritual gifts. As I was going to the church downtown, I passed through a park in the center of the campus of the University of Melbourne. It was very dark all around, except for one well-lit statue. But I could see that statue clearly, and it was beautiful! It was so beautiful, in fact, that as I drove through the park I just had to twist my head around to look at it because I was so attracted to its beauty.

I got to the other side of the park, still thinking about what I had seen. All of a sudden it dawned on me how dark that park was, and how bright that statue was, and how impossible it would have been for me to see that statue apart from the bank of lights that shone on it. Yet, as I was going through the park, not once did I ever focus on the lights and say, "What fantastic lights those are!" This says to me that those lights were really doing their job. Some lights don't light up anything; they just draw attention to themselves. Other lights, however, focus on the object that is to be seen, and you are really unaware of them because you are absorbed with what they are illuminating.

That is exactly what God the Holy Spirit does in faithfulness to His job in the trinity. The Spirit of God does not have the desire to start a Holy Spirit movement. The Spirit of God has only the desire to focus on Jesus Christ.

And the more clearly I see Jesus, the more the Spirit of God is honored—because then He knows that He is doing His job.

That is what Paul was saying. No man speaking by the Spirit of God will ever pull Jesus down, will ever demean Jesus—either directly or indirectly. He will always exalt Jesus. That is why, when you come to the New Testament, every picture of the church has Jesus Christ on center stage. He is the Chief Cornerstone of the building. He is the High Priest over the priesthood. He is the Good, Great, and Chief Shepherd of the flock. He is the Vine of which we are the branches. He is the Head of which we are the body members.

Not one picture of the church of Jesus Christ ever puts the Spirit of God in center stage. Why? Because that is not where the Spirit of God wants to be. He wants to be where He can shine the light in such a way that our attention is focused on the Lord Jesus.

If you want to honor the Spirit of God, therefore, the best way is to imitate His dependence upon the Son of God, and to demonstrate that dependence in your

The Pattern of Dependence

life (Matthew 28:20; John 14:21). And that will please God the Father, God the Son, and God the Spirit.

In the light of this principle, have you noticed the current tendency to emphasize the symbol of the dove rather than the cross? Think about it.

2

THE POWER FOR WITNESS

Having a pattern for living is basic and foundational. In the preceding chapter we discussed the pattern of submission and dependency given by the Holy Spirit. This model will be of great value as we contemplate His other ministries in the believer. Just before Christ ascended, He said:

> *But you shall receive power when the Holy Spirit has come upon you; and you shall be My witnesses both in Jerusalem, and in all Judea and Samaria, and even to the remotest part of the earth.*
>
> *–Acts 1:8*

This verse adds a significant dimension to the Great Commission: the Holy Spirit would empower believers to fulfill it. But that commission often gets choked out because of weeds the devil puts in our path. The seeds of two of these weeds are mentioned in the passage surrounding Acts 1:8.

Jesus had spent years preparing His disciples for the commission He would leave with them. But when they came together just before His ascension, the issue foremost in their minds was a *time* rather than a *mission*.

Much the same thing took place at the upper room discourse, when Jesus said, in essence, "I am going to leave you. You cannot go with Me, but I have something very important to tell you that is going to be the key to your outreach." Then He gave them that tremendous statement:

> *"A new commandment I give to you, that you love one another, even as I have loved you, that you also love one another. By this all men will know that you are My disciples, if you have love for one another."*
> *-John 13:34, 35*

The Lord Jesus had no more than finished the sentence when Peter took Him back to His previous statement that He was going to leave, and that they could not go with Him. Peter's question was, "Lord, where are You going? Why can I not follow You right now?" (John 13:36, 37). Like so many of us, Peter missed the main point.

By the way, we are still missing that point today in evangelism, because most of our efforts are focused on the lost. The clue Jesus gave, however, was that the lost were going to get saved as the saved got saved.

Let me explain. Those who have been saved from the *penalty of sin* (justification) need to go on being

The Power for Witness

saved from the *power of sin* (sanctification). As the saved focus on one another and love one another, this will precipitate the lost getting saved. But we stumble over that again and again. Peter stumbled over it. He missed it—at least at that point—consciously.

In Acts 1 we observe that the disciples stumbled and missed it again. The question paramount in their minds was, Lord, is it now? They said, "Lord, is it at this time You are restoring the kingdom to Israel?" (Acts 1:6).

That eschatological problem was not locked into one generation. It has come down, for almost 2,000 years. I hate to say it, but I think that many of my brethren, men with whom I solidly agree both theologically and eschatologically, are asking the same question the disciples asked: "Is it at this time?" If a person writes a book today giving the time of Christ's coming, he can almost guarantee that it will be a bestseller. Even though people have been fooled time and again, they will keep investing money in someone's speculations.

I listened briefly the other day to a radio broadcast by a man in Southern California. I was amazed that he still has a program, because several years ago he published a book predicting that Jesus was going to come on Labor Day of 1976. I remember a lot of people asking me, "Do you really think it is true?" I responded, "No, it is garbage!" After that holiday in 1976, needless to say, there was not a very great call for that book. The author, I am sure, was eager to retrieve all the copies he could. But he is still on the air, and he is still promoting the same ideas. One man who was an ardent supporter of that book and a strong pretribulationist is now a posttribulationist. He tells us that he has learned through that experience that the pretribulation view is wrong. Preposterous!

More recently there was another author and radio Bible teacher who predicted that Jesus would return on May 21, 2011. Millions of dollars flowed into his ministry bank account to help him spread the word. Some people quit their jobs, sold their houses, and sent in all their life savings. When Jesus did not return on May 21, he claimed that Jesus did actually return and the world did actually end, but it was a "spiritual end." He then went on to predict that the world would physically end on October 21, 2011. That didn't happen either, but most surprisingly of all, this radio Bible teacher is still on the air and people still send in money to support his ministry.

Date-setters have been active since Jesus left the earth, and Christians still cannot seem to kick the habit. Sometimes they start off by saying, "I know that we are not supposed to set dates, but ..." It is the word "but" that bothers me. A friend of mine, calls it the motorboat problem—the "but, but, but, but, but" problem.

When Anwar Sadat and Menachem Begin got together, phone calls were racing all over the country: "Is this a fulfillment of prophecy?" I answered one caller by saying, "This is not a sign of the times, because we are not in the time of the signs." He said, "I beg your pardon. Would you bring that back again, please?" I responded, "This is not a sign of the times, because we are not in the time of the signs." He answered, "I never heard that before." And I said, "Well, I suggest you think it through."

The Power for Witness

On another occasion, I was debating with a friend of mine who is a posttribulationist. At the end of our discussion, I said, "You know, if I supported your viewpoint, I believe I would have capitalized a little more on a verse that you just briefly mentioned. It is part of Jesus' prayer to His Father in John 17, 'I do not ask Thee to take them out of the world, but to keep them from the evil one.'" I went on, "I make that suggestion to you because I think that some of us—some of my brethren who hold the premillennial viewpoint—are more interested in getting out of a corrupt and perverse world than they are in reaching it." But if that is the case, why did God send us into it in the first place?

I take the Bible to teach that my primary task is not to get out of the world, but to reach it. Don't get me wrong. I am just as interested in Christ's coming as anybody. I am fully aware that I could be raptured before I finish writing this paragraph. I am truly anticipating the imminent return of the Lord Jesus. But I think we need to beware lest we make the same mistake the disciples did in Acts 1—being more consumed with escaping this world than reaching it. With the population explosion we are experiencing today, we ought to be excited to the end of our toes with the potential of reaching people for Christ.

I remember a prophecy conference in which a man came up to me after a message and verbally chastised me for encouraging the congregation to pray for revival. He said, "The Bible teaches that the Lord is going to come in dark days; but, if you keep telling people to pray for revival and revival happens, you are going to defer the coming of the Lord." My friend, that is prophecy gone to seed!

The disciples said, "Is it now, Lord? Is it now?" And He said, "It is not for you to know." The disciples were not quite over that yet, because after He had ascended they were still standing there gazing into the sky. So the angels asked them, "Why do you stand here staring off into space? Why do you not get on with what He told you to do?" While the followers of Jesus were gazing heavenward, they were missing the Great Commission. One of the problems we face today is keeping a balance in our theology between our ecclesiology (doctrine of the church), our eschatology (doctrine of last things), and our soteriology (doctrine of salvation).

The next phrase of Acts 1:8 contains the seed of another weed that we face again today. Christ said, "But you shall receive power." Many times people stop there and say, "Oh yes! I have access to power." We tend to interpret this promise as receiving some kind of personal power for living by faith. We get together in our little groups and spiritually massage one another with the awareness that the power we have was not available in the days before Pentecost. We need to be careful, however, with some inferences we make about Old Testament saints.

When I read the account of the heroes of the faith in Hebrews 11, I become a little hesitant to talk much about contemporary demonstrations of power. For example, a man named Joseph got trapped into a compromising situation with Potiphar's wife (Genesis 39). She said, "Come to bed with me." But he refused.

"With me in charge," he told her, "my master does not concern himself with anything in the house; everything he owns he has entrusted to my care. No one is greater in this house than I am. My master has withheld nothing from me except you, because you are his wife. How then could I do such a wicked thing and sin against God?"

~ Genesis 39:8-9 (NIV)

Day after day this woman worked at seducing Joseph. Finally, she grabbed his garment and said, "Come to bed with me!" He pulled away from her and ran, leaving his garment in her hand. I have the idea that God and His power were at work in Joseph's life. I could wish that some of us today who claim to have so much power for living would have the sense to run from compromising situations. But it seems from the moral situation today (even within evangelicalism) we do not have the good sense to run in spite of all our Spirit-filled power.

Again, I could wish that we would see power in our lives today like Abraham had when he took his son, his only son Isaac, to sacrifice him in obedience to God (Genesis 22). Although he intended to slay his son, he said, "We will worship and return to you" (Genesis 22:5). Somehow the patriarch had the ability to believe in a God who raises people from the dead (see Hebrews 11:19).

I could wish that we would demonstrate with all of our power the kind of resolution that was seen in Shadrach, Meshach, and Abed-nego. When I read that story, goose-bumps come to my skin as I think of the challenge those young men faced. They had a firm, accurate grasp of what their God was like. The king said:

> *"Is it true, Shadrach, Meshach, and Abed-nego, that you do not serve my gods or worship the golden image that I have set up?*
>
> *"Now if you are ready, at the moment you hear the sound of the horn, flute, lyre, trigon, psaltery, and bagpipe, and all kinds of music, to fall down and worship the image that I have made, very well. But if you will not worship, you will immediately be cast into the midst of a furnace of blazing fire; and what god is there who can deliver you out of my hands?"*
> ~Daniel 3:14-15

Then we're told how the young men responded:

> *Shadrach, Meshach, and Abed-nego answered and said to the king, "O Nebuchadnezzar, we do not need to give you an answer concerning this.*
>
> *"If it be so, our God whom we serve is able to deliver us from the furnace of blazing fire; and He will deliver us out of your hand, O king.*
>
> *"But even if He does not, let it be known to you, O king, that we are not going to serve your gods or worship the golden image that you have set up."*
> ~Daniel 3:16-18

The king had said the wrong thing, because Shadrach, Meshach, and Abed-nego had no question about their

The Power for Witness

God. They boldly replied, "Our God is *able* to deliver. The only question is if He will or not. So let us have at it and see what He will do." Oh, that we had such resolution today!

Go on to think of Daniel in the lion's den, Isaiah, Joshua, and other heroes of the Old Testament. Then hear people say they have a kind of personal power that people did not have in those times. It cannot be!

The problem is that these people stopped reading too soon in the verse (Acts 1:8). The text says, "But you shall receive power when the Holy Spirit has come upon you; and you shall be My witnesses …" *The power was for witnessing!* That element was distinct from what had taken place before. Israel was not a people who witnessed. True, there were times when they did (see Isaiah 43). But basically, Israel was called to be the vehicle of special revelation. Through its writers and leaders would come the law and the prophets. Preeminently, through Israel would come the Seed. God kept the nation separate so separate that when they disobeyed Him and married Gentiles in the Babylonian captivity, He demanded that they divorce these pagan brides. A divine order to divorce has never happened in our age, nor has it been, commanded for today. But in this instance divorce was commanded by the Lord—to keep Israel pure, because they were preparing something. And in the fullness of the time, through Israel, God finally brought the Redeemer into the world.

Now we come to the important occasion of Acts 1. It took place just before the formation of the grandest organism God has ever created on earth, the church. (We will talk more about that later.) But in the transition—a dramatic transition as God moved from the use of Israel as His mediatorial people on the earth to the use of the church (preeminently Gentiles) as His mediatorial people on the earth—Jesus Christ has prepared the foundation stones of the church. Here in Acts 1, He is setting before the disciples their mission. They could not have had any idea of how monumental their assigned task would be.

When Jesus was speaking to His disciples, perhaps 200 million people were living on the earth. I am sure His followers had a very small concept of the dimensions of the planet. They could not possibly have had any idea that at some generation down the line, over 7 billion people would inhabit the earth. It was not until the 19th century that earth reached its first billion in population—a billion people that would live somewhere forever! Then, after two-thirds of a century, we had another billion; in one-third of a century, we had another billion. And now, in the 21st century, we have surpassed 7 billion people!

When you look out on the earth and see all of the horror and evil, do you also see people—people who will live forever? Sometimes I feel welling up within me, rather than the revelation cry, "Come quickly, Lord Jesus," the words, "God, give us a little more time. God, stir us up. God, do not allow us to be numbed by the lethargy and indolence of our day. Don't let us see people walking by us going to either heaven or hell (we know not which until we know them) and yet not be bothered enough to tell them about Christ."

The Power for Witness

One of the things for which I thank God about my college training is that there was constant pressure on us to get out and tell people about Jesus Christ—because they are either lost or they are saved. If they are lost and they die like that, they will spend eternity in separation from Jesus Christ in a place called hell. We need to think carefully about that in our day as well.

The uniqueness of the church, then, was that it would be made up of witnessing people with an opportunity the likes of which had never been on planet earth. They did not know it at that time, but Jesus knew it. When He gave that commission, He knew century twenty just as well as century one.

It is not for you to know times or epochs which the Father has fixed by His own authority; but you shall receive power when the Holy Spirit has come upon you (Acts 1:7-8). Power for what? "You shall be My witnesses." Interestingly enough, that is exactly what the apostles did. After the expression of the sign-gifts of Acts—those things given during that dramatic transition time which showed that God was moving away from the nation of Israel as His mediatorial people and to the church—the disciples spoke the Word of God clearly and without fear as a witness for Jesus Christ. From that point on, when the followers of Christ are spoken of as being filled with the Spirit, it is in connection with statements like Peter made in Acts 4:

> *"Rulers and elders of the people, if we are on trial today for a benefit done to a sick man, as to how this man has been made well, let it be known to all of you, and to all the people of Israel, that by the name of Je-*

> *sus Christ the Nazarene, whom you crucified, whom God raised from the dead—by this name this man stands here before you in good health. He is the stone which was rejected by you, the builders, but which became the very cornerstone. And there is salvation in no one else; for there is no other name under heaven that has been given among men, by which we must be saved."*
>
> *Now as they observed the confidence of Peter and John, and understood that they were uneducated and untrained men, they were marveling, and began to recognize them as having been with Jesus.*
> *-Acts 4:8-13*

That was the power! Now the disciples could stand up and speak without intimidation and with good sense. Before, Peter had been impulsive when he whipped out his sword (see John 18:10). His aim was not too good, but at least he had some boldness. Even so, he did not yet understand who Jesus Christ really was.

Jesus had given Peter a little insight by telling him what His potential kill-power was at that point. "Do you not realize I could call on 72,000 angels right now?" One angel in the Old Testament killed 185,000 people; so, if you multiply 72,000 times 185,000, you get an estimate of the kill-power at Jesus' disposal. But no, Jesus was not talking about that kind of power at all.

When Peter was intimidated by the crowd, he pulled out his sword. But when you come to Acts 4, Peter did not respond that way anymore. The officials

The Power for Witness

said, "Do not speak in the name of Jesus again" (Acts 4:18). They hated Jesus so much they did not want to even hear the mention of His name. "Do not speak in. that name again." But this time Peter did not pull out his sword and say, "Oh, yeah? You and who else is going to stop me, you big bullies? Try it!" No, Peter was fearless, secure, and confident. He said to himself, in essence, "I will speak this message of the resurrected Christ, and nobody will lay a hand on me unless the Sovereign God allows it. And if the Sovereign God allows it, I am ready to check out of life and go to be with Him." What a difference between Peter in the last chapters of John, and Peter in the first chapters of Acts!

The difference was also demonstrated in the boldness with which the apostles spoke the Word of God. Back in the upper room discourse, Jesus had told the disciples that He was going to give them boldness. He had told them that the Holy Spirit was going to empower them for witness. But they were taken up with their own sorrows, their own world situation, and the threat of death. Let me paraphrase what Jesus had said to them, "They are going to kick you out of the synagogues. They hate you, and they are going to kill you, and they are going to think they are doing God a service in killing you." While that message was still fresh in their minds, Jesus said to them, "I am going to leave you." But then He went on to say, "I am going to send you another Helper." And what was the Helper going to do? The answer is in John 15.

> *When the Helper comes, whom I will send to you from the Father, that is the Spirit of truth, who proceeds*

> *from the Father, He will bear witness of Me, and you will bear witness also, because you have been with Me from the beginning."*
>
> *-John 15:26-27*

The peculiar work of the Holy Spirit, therefore, was to be a witness for the case of Jesus Christ.

Perhaps this parallel will help. In 1 John 2:1 we are taught that Jesus is our helper at the right hand of the Father. Yes, He is my *parakletos*; He is my defense attorney there. When the devil makes accusation against me, Jesus, who paid the price for my sins, who shed His blood for me, is there to plead my case. He is my defense attorney. The same word that is used for the work of Jesus, who paid the price for my sins, who shed His blood for me, is there to plead my case. He is my defense attorney. The same word that is used for the work of Jesus on my behalf at the right hand of the Father is used here of the Holy Spirit. When I witness, He is at my right hand, so to speak, on behalf of Jesus Christ.

Jesus Christ has a defense attorney resident in me and in every believer—the Holy Spirit. The work of the Holy Spirit is to make a case for Jesus Christ in the world through me. That case is spelled out in John 16. Read the introductory statement, where Jesus said:

> *"But I tell you the truth, it is to your advantage that I go away; for if I do not go away, the Helper [the Spirit of truth, the advocate] shall not come to you; but if I go, I will send Him to you.*

The Power for Witness

> *"And He, when He comes, will convict the world [that is, He will demonstrate to the world in a clear light beyond fear of contradiction] concerning sin, and righteousness, and judgment"*
>
> *~John 16:7-8*

The Word of God says that the Spirit of God is going to work on those three things—sin, righteousness, and judgment—through the believer. He is going to make a case for Jesus Christ through the believer to the world. When I encounter an unsaved person, it excites me to realize that I am not there on my own. I do not find it any easier than a lot of other believers to talk to people about Jesus Christ without fear. But I am helped because I recognize what God is doing. God the Holy Spirit has promised me that if I will get my mind thinking right about the elements that He wants to convict the world about, and if my mouth will verbalize those truths, I can count on this truth: when I talk to that person, God the Holy Spirit will empower that witness. He will be reinforcing it. True, He is not going to be giving content that I do not have. But when I give content that is faithful to the Word of God, the Spirit is in essence going to be reinforcing that content in the inner life of that person. He will be saying, "It is true. You had better believe it. It is true." He does this so that no man will ever go through this world without having had the witness of the Holy Spirit. The Spirit-filled believer who knows the Word of God has the power to witness to people in the world today.

When I witness for Christ, I not only know the Word with which to witness, but I also know that another, a divine attorney, is making a case for Jesus Christ. The Holy Spirit is saying to that unsaved person, "Friend, you had better believe it. You had better believe it because it is the truth." The cultists, the false religionists, have no such asset. Only the believer in Jesus Christ has it. "You shall receive power when the Holy Spirit has come upon you; and you shall be My witnesses." Jerusalem, Judea, Samaria, the uttermost part of the earth, and 7 billion people today. Do we care?

3

THE PROTECTOR OF THE CHURCH

The subject we come to now has probably been more controversial and divisive within evangelical Christianity than any other particular topic. It is the doctrine often referred to as the baptism of the Holy Spirit.

We have moved from the pattern to the power, and now we go on to consider the protection by the Spirit of God in the unique organism called the "church," the body of Christ. This is really what baptism in the Spirit is all about.

I am going to interpret and discuss a number of verses of Scripture. I trust that this discussion will not become overly technical; however, I do want it to be technical enough to be sure that we do not miss what the Scripture says. We need to see the clear distinction between what has been foisted upon the Scripture about the baptism in the Holy Spirit, and what it actually teaches. For example, the phrase, "the baptism of the Holy Spirit," is a nonscriptural phrase. No such statement appears in the Word of God. It is a theological formulation that has been made as a result of some people's interpretation of scriptural data, but these words do not appear in the Bible.

In order for you to see that, I would like to have you take a careful look at the seven statements in Scripture that specifically refer to this topic. Before an adequate doctrine of Spirit baptism can be developed, we need to look at each occurrence of the statement in its biblical context. Four of the seven occurrences are in the gospels, two are in Acts, and one is in 1 Corinthians. Five of the seven are prophetical at the time of their statement, two are historical, and one is doctrinal.

Let us begin by reading the setting of the first statement, found in John 1.

> *John answered them saying, "I baptize in water, but among you stands One whom you do not know. It is He who comes after me, the thong of whose sandal I am not worthy to untie. And I did not recognize Him, but in order that He might be manifested to Israel, I came baptizing in water."*
>
> *And John bore witness saying, "I have beheld the Spirit descending as a dove out of heaven, and He remained upon Him. And I did not recognize Him, but He who sent me to baptize in water said to me, 'He upon whom you see the Spirit descending and remaining upon Him, this is the one who baptizes in the Holy Spirit.'" ~John 1:26-27, 31-33*

The Protector of the Church

Something first must be said about the word "baptize." The word "baptize" was familiar in John's day in a nontheological, nontechnical sense as a trade word. It was a word that Lydia, the seller of purple, would have been familiar with. This is because she (or her employees) regularly practiced the process it described when she would dip a piece of unbleached cloth into a vat of purple and then remove it. That act would have been referred to by the Greek verb *baptizō*, from which we transliterate the English word "baptize."

I think we can all agree that "baptism" is not a translation; rather, it is simply a transliteration. I suppose the translators did not want to get into the hassle of taking sides about the interpretation, so they did not bother to translate this word. They just transliterated it, and unfortunately they left the problem of interpretation to people afterward.

To place a piece of cloth into that vat of dye, therefore, was to baptize. And when the cloth was removed, it was identified in color with the dye in the vat. A consequent meaning of the term "baptize," then, came to be "identification." This has often been called the metaphorical usage of the term; namely, it is "to be identified with." The color of the cloth was identical with the color in the vat. Identity or identification was a basic idea in the word long before it was given a theological usage.

When John came baptizing, then, the people who heard his message and responded to it participated in a symbolic act of dipping or being placed into water. But that act signified something even more—their identification with the message that John the Baptist was preaching. When they allowed themselves to be baptized by him, they were identifying themselves with his message. "I baptize you," he said, "in water. There comes One who shall baptize you in the Holy Spirit." He was telling them that another act of identification was forthcoming.

One other technical matter needs clarification. In the *New American Standard Bible* translation, alongside the occurrences of the words "baptize in water" and "baptize in the Holy Spirit," is a little note that says, "The Greek here can be translated 'in,' 'with,' or 'by.'" This comment refers to the little Greek preposition *en*, which appears more than 2,400 times in the New Testament. In the vast majority of cases, it is simply rendered "in." It regularly occurs with the locative case, which answers the question "where?" Its key idea, therefore, is "place." Now, the translations vary by using "with," "by," or "in" for the word *en* in these parallel passages on water baptism and Spirit baptism. Even so, the fact is that the Greek preposition does not vary. The reason therefore eludes me why my translation should use "in" throughout the passage in John and then, when the same preposition is used in the parallel passages in Matthew, Mark, and Luke, the translator used "with." This must be confusing to the reader. In any event, it would be far more consistent to translate this word with the English preposition "in" in each of the seven passages that refer to Spirit baptism. All of this may not seem significant, but it will pick up meaning as we move along.

John therefore said, in essence, "I baptize you in water, for you are identified with me and the message that

The Protector of the Church

I preach. There is another One coming who shall baptize you in the Holy Spirit, and you will then be identified with the organism He inaugurates and the message He proclaims." The idea, then, is "placement into" and "consequent identification with." The sphere into which John was placing his followers was water; the sphere into which Christ would be placing them was the Spirit.

Notice next that the agent of baptism in the four parallel references in Matthew, Mark, Luke, and John is Jesus Christ. I emphasize that point because we often hear of the baptism of the Holy Spirit or the baptism by the Holy Spirit. May I suggest this to your thought: using that terminology takes the focus away from the One on whom the focus is to be placed. Jesus Christ is the Head of the church. He is the One who places people in the body. The Spirit of God does the bidding of the Son of God, who is to have the preeminence.

I take it, therefore, that the agent of this baptism is Jesus Christ. His is the message with which they are identified. His would be the organism they would later become a part of—the church. And it is by Jesus Christ that they are put into the organism *in the Spirit*, and identified with Christ. In summary, then, the objects of the baptism are those who identify themselves with Christ and His message. The agent of this baptism is Jesus Christ. And the sphere within which the baptized are placed is the Holy Spirit. Let me rephrase that last statement. Those who through faith in Christ have been declared to be "in Christ" are, by Christ, placed into a "body" relationship. They are put in the Spirit for His care and safekeeping.

What to Expect from the Holy Spirit

We will now look at several additional key references in John. The first appears in John chapter 7. We read:

> *Now on the last day, the great day of the feast, Jesus stood and cried out, saying, "If any man is thirsty, let him come to Me and drink. He who believes in Me, as the Scripture said, 'From his innermost being shall flow rivers of living water.'*
>
> *But this He spoke of the Spirit, whom those who believed in Him were to receive; for the Spirit was not yet given, because Jesus was not yet glorified.*
> ~John 7:37-39

A beautiful parallel to that passage is found in the prophecy of Jeremiah.

> *Blessed is the man who trusts in the Lord*
> *And whose trust is the Lord.*
> *For he will be like a tree planted by the water,*
> *That extends its roots by a stream*
> *And will not fear when the heat comes;*
> *But its leaves will be green,*
> *And it will not be anxious in a year of drought*
> *Nor cease to yield fruit.*
> ~Jeremiah 17:7-8

In John 7, the Lord was referring to the waters mentioned by Jeremiah. I take it that the rivers of living water that come forth from me are the Scriptures that have been given by the Spirit of God through holy apostles of God. That Word of God, as it is empowered

The Protector of the Church

and reinforced by the Spirit of God coming forth from me, not only invigorates me, but it invigorates those with whom I share it.

This living water is therefore not some kind of mystical nectar out there someplace; rather, that which we eat and drink of the Lord is His Word. At this point, God has nothing else for sanctifying the believer but His Word. That is the reason He prayed, "Sanctify them in the truth; Thy word is truth" (John 17:17). The Word of God is like living water springing up from within me. It has been planted there by the exercise of study—diligent study—in the Word of God, and it is reinforced by the Spirit of God.

John said this of the rivers of living water: "But this He spoke of the Spirit, whom those who believed in Him were to receive; for the Spirit was not yet given, because Jesus was not yet glorified" (John 7:39). You may be saying in your mind, "Now wait a minute. He just said that was the Word of God." But let me caution you. The Spirit of God does not work apart from the Word of God, and the Word of God does not work apart from the Spirit of God. The Spirit of God apart from the Word of God is mute. He has nothing to say. The Word of God apart from the Spirit of God is lifeless. It has no power to act. The Word of God approached apart from the Spirit of God easily leads to mechanicalism. And the Spirit of God approached apart from the Word of God easily leads to fanaticism. But the Word of God conjoined with the Spirit of God will always spell victory in a believer's life.

The Word of God, therefore, is the raw material that the Spirit of God uses to form Jesus Christ in me.

A beautiful coming together of those elements is seen in 2 Corinthians 3:18, where we read that as we reflect on the glory of the Lord we are transformed, transfigured (metamorphosed, if you please) into the same image. What image? The image of the glory of God—Jesus Christ. This is the goal of the true believer. We are "transformed into the same image from glory to glory, just as from the Lord, the Spirit."

So, as I reflect deeply on the Word of God and take it in, that becomes the raw material the Spirit of God uses to form Jesus Christ in me. And the formation of Jesus Christ in me is the Holy Spirit's grandest desire. He wants to have Christ reflected in me. Jesus told the disciples that there was more resource coming for them in this area than they had ever been aware of.

When we get to John 14, we receive a little more information about this Helper. Jesus said: "And I will ask the Father, and He will give you another Helper, that He may be with you forever" (John 14:16). The Spirit of God always works in the area of truth.

> *That is the Spirit of truth, whom the world cannot receive, because it does not behold Him or know Him, but you know Him because He abides with you, and will be in you.*
>
> *–John 14:17*

Keep these verses in mind as you turn to John 20.

> *Jesus therefore said to them again, "Peace be with you; as the Father has sent Me, I also send you."*

> *And when He had said this, He [Christ] breathed on them, and said to them, "Receive the Holy Spirit"*
> *~John 20:21-22*

Jesus had told His followers that the Holy Spirit would be with them and in them. The One who said "He will be in you" is the very One who put the Spirit in them. The disciples were not quite ready for their mission yet. Even though Christ had said, "Receive the Holy Spirit" and had placed the Spirit in them (I take it to be a permanent possession), a little later they in turn were going to be placed in the Spirit.

Look at the first chapter of Acts.

> *And gathering them together, He commanded them not to leave Jerusalem, but to wait for what the Father had promised, "Which," He said, "you heard of from Me; For John baptized with [en] water, but you shall be baptized with* [en] *the Holy Spirit not many days from now."*
>
> *~Acts 1:4-5*

I want to emphasize verse 5. It speaks of something that was yet future when Jesus spoke. "You shall be baptized with [*en*] the Holy Spirit not many days from now."

The next reference to the baptism in the Spirit is in Acts 11:15. Peter was explaining to the disciples at Jerusalem the experience he had had at the house of Cornelius.

> *And as I began to speak, the Holy Spirit fell upon them, just as He did upon us at the beginning.*

WHAT TO EXPECT FROM THE HOLY SPIRIT

And I remembered the word of the Lord, how He used to say, "John baptized with [en] *water, but you shall be baptized with* [en] *the Holy Spirit."*
~Acts 11:15-16

Peter took as his reference point the five prophetic statements about the Holy Spirit in the gospels and in Acts 1.

No mention was made to this baptism between Acts 1 and Acts 11. If it was still future in Acts 1, and if it was past in Acts 11, then whatever this event was, it had to transpire between Acts 1 and Acts 11. The only occasion of such magnitude is in Acts 2. This key passage records the outward demonstration which gave evidence of a momentous occurrence, but it tells us nothing about its doctrinal meaning. In the account of the Day of Pentecost in Acts 2, we have reference to the filling of the Spirit. This was the outwardly experienced demonstration of the momentous, historical, never-to-be-repeated transaction that took place in that upper room.

In our day, some have supposed that the phenomenon in Acts 2 was the baptism in the Holy Spirit—with the focus being on the Holy Spirit and upon the experience. Interestingly enough, many people who believe this have completely overlooked the grandest thing that happened in Acts 2—the birthday of the greatest organism that has ever come upon this earth, the church. The church is the body of Christ, and it is headed by Jesus Christ. Once again, religious men have succeeded in taking the focus off Jesus Christ and putting it on the Holy Spirit. But the Holy Spirit would never wish to have that done!

Many have placed the focus of Pentecost upon the Spirit of God, but the Spirit of God made Pentecost focus on the church, which is headed by Jesus Christ. It is time we got in line with the Spirit of God. How do I know that? I do not have to dream about it or wonder about it, because I can go from the historical event in Acts 2 to the doctrinal exposition of it in First and Second Corinthians and Ephesians.

We have altogether too many piecemeal theologians today. These are people who pick up a piece of Scripture here and a piece of Scripture there. They then proceed to form their own theology, without ever getting the overview of the entirety of the Scriptures. May they read James 3:1, memorize it, and stand on it before the judgment seat of Christ. "Let not many of you become teachers, my brethren," James said, "knowing that as such we shall incur a stricter judgment." God holds us accountable for the teaching, for the doctrine, of the Word of God.

With that in mind, let us note the careful explanation of Pentecost that Paul gave us in 1 Corinthians 12:12, 13, the seventh of the passages of Scripture we are analyzing in this chapter. The apostle was speaking of spiritual gifts, and he began the discussion by giving a metaphor of the church, the body of Christ. In verse 12 he said:

> *For even as the body is one and yet has many members, and all the members of the body, though they are*

many, are one body, so also is Christ.–1 Corinthians 12:12

The most popular metaphor of the church in the Bible is the human body. That is a picture we cannot miss, because all have one. The vine and the branches—we may get confused on that metaphor because we do not understand Judean viticulture. But we cannot get confused on the body. We look at it every day. We pamper it; we work with it. We recognize its diversity. We also recognize its unity. And God chose to use the human body as the most strategic metaphor of the church. He said, "... as the body is one and yet has many members, and all the members of the body, though they are many, are one body, so also is Christ."

After making this analogy, Paul gave us a birthday notice in 1 Corinthians 12:13: "For by [*en*] one Spirit" [that is, in the sphere of one Spirit] "we were all baptized into one body, whether Jews or Greeks, whether slaves or free, and we were all made to drink of one Spirit." May I bring it to your attention that when Paul explained this doctrinally, he did not say we were baptized into the Spirit. Rather, he said we were baptized into one body. That is the essence of it! That is also the uniqueness of it! Jesus Christ died, was buried, was raised again, and ascended to the right hand of the Father. His first act as the ascended, exalted Lord was to inaugurate His church, the body of Christ. The Head then began to gather around Himself a body. And what was the raw material He used? He used Jew and Gentile; furthermore, of all things, He put them together in one body!

That had to be a miracle! For centuries the Jews had been told that they were the people of God. Amos recorded that. Other prophets recorded it as well. The Lord God said, "You only have I chosen among all the families of the earth" (Amos 3:2). The Jews had looked upon the Gentiles as barbarian dogs. Now Gentiles were coming along and saying they were the people of God. The typical Jew would say, "You must have checked your brain out to lunch. Have you never read the Bible? Do you not know that we are the people of God? We are the ones through whom have come the law, the prophets, and the writings—not the Gentiles." Furthermore, if a Gentile were to be rightly related to God, he would have to become a "God-fearer," a Jewish proselyte. All of a sudden, however, in God's great providence, the tables were turned. The people the Jews looked down upon, the Gentiles, the people who were not a people, became the people of God. The natural branches of the tree of Romans 11 were broken off (not for all time and not entirely) and the wild branches, the Gentiles, were grafted in. God did a brand-new thing.

Now that was hard for the Jews to accept. God therefore did some miraculous things by way of sign-gifts to get their attention. He had prophesied that He would in Isaiah 28:11-12, and Paul spoke of the fulfillment in 1 Corinthians 14:21. The Lord got the Jews' attention. Even so, they did not believe. The Bible plainly says in 1 Corinthians 14:21 that the use of the sign-gifts did not bring about an evangelistic result in Israel. The Jews did not believe; even so, God got their attention. It was like the farmer out in the pasture hitting his mule over the head with a two-by-four. When they asked him what he was trying to do, he said that he was only trying to get his mule's attention. God has used some strange means to get people's attention.

But God did get the Jews' attention. In that traumatic transition in history, with all of the signs recorded in Acts 2 and referred to in chapters 10 and 19, the Lord said, in essence, "I am turning from you. And I am turning to this people that you looked upon as not a people. And in this period of time, I am going to do a new thing on the earth. I am going to take Jew and Gentile, and I am going to put them together in one body. I am not going to make Gentiles out of Jews or Jews out of Gentiles, but I am going to take My church from both. I am going to put together in one body those who have been separated by a middle wall of partition. That will be a miracle to behold" (see Ephesians 2:11–3:12).

That is what Paul was talking about in 1 Corinthians 12:13. We were all, in the sphere of one Spirit, placed into one body by Jesus Christ. The Spirit of God, then (in 1 Corinthians 12:13, as well as in the other six references), is the sphere in which the Head of the body, Jesus Christ, places this new body called the "church." For what purpose? For its care and safekeeping by the Spirit until the time when the Head will be reunited with the body at the rapture.

The Spirit of God has the desire to bring unity to that body. This is not merely unity in theory, but unity in practice. The doctrine of the "in Spirit" baptism into the body, when properly understood and applied, produces unity—not disunity, not divisiveness— in the grand organism called the "church." Consequently, as believers moved out to witness for Jesus Christ, there would be an undistorted reflection of their Head, the Lord Jesus.

As an application of this truth, consider Ephesians 4, where Paul spoke of the attitude that is to be maintained by this one body. He said:

Being diligent to preserve the unity of the Spirit in the bond of peace. There is one body and one Spirit, just as also you were called in one hope of your calling; one Lord, one faith, one baptism, one God and Father of all who is over all and through all and in all
~Ephesians 4:3-6

The apostle was saying that as I come to the one Lord, Jesus Christ, there is a single message of faith by which I own Him as Lord—one Lord, one faith, one baptism—and by which Christ places us in body relationship. In like fashion, in our local churches, which are the microcosm of the macrocosm (the smaller of the larger), we go through the symbolism of baptism. By this we identify openly with what Christ has already done by our response to Him in faith. "One Lord, one faith, one baptism." Christ baptizes us; He places us into the body, His body, in the care of the Spirit. We in turn evidence the truth of that by submitting to baptism into a local church, and then by subjecting ourselves to do and practice everything Jesus taught.

The key element that will bring unity to local churches is submission to the God-ordained leadership of that church. We therefore should choose the church we attend in submission to the Head of the church,

Jesus Christ, and in the strength of the Spirit of God (see Hebrews 13:17).

We have considered a much-debated doctrine in a short space. Let us not forget that Jesus Christ placed us into one body, in the sphere of the Spirit, in order that we should preserve the unity of the Spirit. Thereby we would reflect Jesus Christ so attractively that when people look at His church they will have their appetites whetted to know the Savior—whom to know is life eternal.

4

THE PROVIDER OF THE GIFTS

The very first words Jesus Christ spoke with respect to His church were remarkable. He said, "I will build My church; and the gates of hades shall not overpower it" (Matthew 16:18). Nothing on earth or under the earth or above the earth will ever be able to destroy the church of Jesus Christ! After the Lord Jesus had paid the price for the church in His death, burial, and resurrection (Paul referred to the church in Acts 20:28 as the "church of God which He purchased with His own blood"), He then ascended to the right hand of the Father. There He took up His exalted position as Head of that church, that unique body of believers that would have its birthday on the Day of Pentecost.

We sought to share with you in the previous chapter that the unique thing which happened at Pentecost was not primarily a ministry of the Holy Spirit. Rather, it was essentially and first the birthday of that grand organism Jesus Christ had announced in Matthew 16, the church. When Paul talked about the doctrine of spiritual gifts and the way they have been distributed, he referred back to the birthday of the church. He said that "[in] one Spirit we were all baptized into one body" (1 Corinthians 12:13).

The New Testament leaves no doubt about what that body is. Ephesians and Colossians repeatedly refer to the church which is His body, and to the body which is His church. The body of Christ is His church. Paul said that we were all, Jew and Gentile, baptized (that is, placed) into one body. The great thing that happened at Pentecost—in that transitional period from God's use of the nation of Israel as His mediatorial people on earth to His use primarily of Gentiles as His mediatorial people on earth—was that a new organism came into being called the "church," the body of Christ. And Pentecost was the birthday of the church.

But Jesus Christ was now ascended into heaven. The Head was absent from the body. He had told them in the upper room that this would happen. "I am going to leave you," He had said. "But I am not going to leave you orphans. I will send another *paracletos*, another Helper. He is with you. He will be in you."

As a matter of fact, Jesus informed us that the Godhead has its presence in the church. "I will not leave you as orphans; I will come to you" (John 14:18). When we hear these words, we often race in our thinking right to the second advent. But do not race too quickly. Jesus then says this:

"After a little while the world will behold Me no more; but you will behold Me; because I live, you shall live also. In that day you shall know that I am in My Father, and you in Me, and I in you."
~John 14:19-20

Then, in verse 23, Jesus said,

"If anyone loves Me, he will keep My word; and My Father will love him, and We [My Father and I] will come to him, and make Our abode with him."
~John 14:23

The fourteenth chapter of John leaves no question about the presence of Father, Son, and Holy Spirit in the life of a believer—in the body of Christ, the church. It also leaves no question about the assignment that has been given to the Spirit of God. The Holy Spirit has been commissioned by the Head of the church, Jesus Christ, to take care of the church. When Jesus said that the gates of hades will not overpower the church, He did not say it lightly. He gave His Spirit charge over the church.

That is why Paul taught in 1 Corinthians 12:13 that the agent of the baptism, Jesus Christ, placed us (Jew and Gentile) into a body relationship. He then placed that body in the sphere of the Spirit for His care and safekeeping until the body would be reunited with the Head at the rapture. So there is no chance that the church will not be taken care of, because the Head of the church, Jesus Christ, has given the Spirit of God the responsibility of taking care of the church; and He will do it. That is the meaning of 1 Corinthians 12:13.

The Spirit of God takes care of the church in some very specific ways. One of those ways is by distributing to the members of the body the gifts that Christ, the ascended Head, has given.

It should be noted that even though we often talk about the gifts being given by the Spirit, Scripture does not say that. The Bible talks about gifts that were given by Christ (Ephesians 4:7-8). The Head of the church makes the assignments for the membership of the church. The Spirit of God, in submission to the Son of God (and I amplify that again because of His example of dependency), distributes gifts to each member of the church as the Lord has assigned (see 1 Corinthians 12:11). The Spirit of God faithfully carries out the assignments of the Son of God, the Head of the church.

An outline of the provisions made for the church by Christ appears in Ephesians 4. Some of the principles He practiced in the formation, organization, and activity of the church were similar to those God used with His former mediatorial people, Israel. Without trying to expound the text in detail, let me call your attention to three important items in Ephesians 4.

OUR CALLING

Most believers have already been taught that the last three chapters of Ephesians are the practical demonstration of the doctrine found in the first three chapters. No chapter in all of God's Word gives a more specific delineation of what the church is really all about than Ephesians 3, which concludes with these words:

> *Now to Him who is able to do exceeding abundantly beyond all that we ask or think, according to the power that works within us, to Him be the glory in the church and in Christ Jesus to all generations forever and ever. Amen*
>
> *-Ephesians 3:20-21*

Having said that, the apostle immediately began chapter 4 by saying, "I, therefore, the prisoner of the Lord, entreat you [beg of you] to walk in a manner worthy of the calling with which you have been called" (Ephesians 4:1). Literally, the word "worthy" means "weighty." It suggests the scales and balances of ancient times. You put the weight on one side and the figs on the other side, and the two should balance. Thus Paul said that, having seen what our high, lofty, holy calling is, we should then walk "weighty" of the calling—let our walk be worthy of the calling we have. In Ephesians 4:1-6, therefore, the apostle gave us our vocation. He said that each of us has a vocation or a calling.

Thankfully, I think we finally have gotten past the age in which people seem to have had the idea that some were called and 'others were not called. They especially thought that the missionary was called. Then, more particularly, they thought the missionary who went across saltwater was called. So they ended up with a very small, exclusive group of Christians who were called. The Scripture knows of no such exclusive group.

There is not a select group of called people within the church. Every member of the body of Christ has the same calling—the same vocation. In the body, not many believers earn their living from this calling. Most people earn their living from an avocation so they can help pay the bills for the others who earn their living from their vocation—their calling. So whether you earn your living from it or not, the fact is that whoever you are, you have a calling in the body of Christ. You have a vocation. And every last member of Jesus Christ has that same call.

Paul explained in the succeeding verses what attitude I ought to maintain in carrying out that calling.

> *There is one body and one Spirit, just as also you were called in one hope of your calling; one Lord, one faith, one baptism, one God and Father of all who is over all and through all and in all.*
> ~*Ephesians 4:4-6*

The baptism that Jesus Christ accomplished spiritually in placing us into a spiritual body, the church, is to have its follow through in the ordinance of baptism that takes place in the local church. That is not another baptism; there is "one baptism." But it has two sides. My baptism into the body of Christ is to be portrayed on the earthly level through the symbolism of the ordinance of local church baptism. So Jesus Christ, the Head, baptizes me into a spiritual body that goes beyond the bounds of any local church. Having become rightly related to the Lord of that body, Jesus Christ, I then vividly portray my relationship to Him, and to my

The Provider of the Gifts

owning of Him as Lord, by submitting to the ordinance that He gave as His first command. I am baptized into a local fellowship of believers called "church."

It is important for us today to understand that even though we theologically may have divided between the visible church and the invisible church, God has not. That notion came out of John Calvin, and before that, out of Augustine. I find too many people today who belong to the "invisible church." The reason I know they belong to the invisible church is because of their invisible attendance and their invisible tithes and their invisible talents. God is not doing His work through the invisible church. He is doing His work through a very visible church, the local church, that has His calling and that has His gifts.

Every person who has been baptized by Christ into the body of Christ, placed into the sphere of the Spirit of God, is now to own up to that. He does so by outwardly identifying himself, with the one Lord of the church through baptism, the vehicle of the ordinance that Jesus Christ gave. Baptism, then, relates a person to a group. Spirit baptism relates him to the entire church, the body of Christ, and the ordinance of baptism relates him to the local church.

Baptism and church membership, then, go together. The consequent accountability is clearly seen in this passage:

> *Obey your leaders, and submit to them; for they keep watch over your souls, as those who will give an account. Let them do this with joy and not with grief,*

for this would be unprofitable for you. -Hebrews 13:17

In the statement of the Great Commission in Matthew 28, we are instructed to disciple the nations. How? By baptizing them, and by teaching them to practice all the principles that Jesus had taught. We are not simply to make decisions; we are to make disciples. In the Scriptures, when people came to Christ they identified with local churches. You do not see disciples in the Bible that are not related to local churches.

To summarize, then, every one of us has a calling we have received from the ascended Lord. We are to know that calling, and we are to practice it in and through a church—the local counterpart of the universal body of Christ.

OUR GIFTS

Second, God has not only given us a calling, but He has also given us gifts. Notice the word "but" that introduces Ephesians 4:7. It indicates that a contrast is being made. "But to each one of us grace was given according to the measure of Christ's gift." The Lord not only gave us a vocation, a calling within the body, He also gave us specific gifts, tools, for carrying out our calling in that body. What tool has He put in your hand? Can you identify it? Do you know what your spiritual gift is?

I suggested in the first chapter that before 1960, very little of worth was written on the doctrine of the

The Provider of the Gifts

spiritual gifts as taught in the Word of God. Since that time, however, we have had a flood of material. More attention has been given to this subject in the last several decades than perhaps at any time since the days of the early church. I wonder, though, if we have become as knowledgeable of our spiritual gifts as they were in the first century.

When the leaders of the early church were looking for people to minister to a particular problem about serving the tables and about providing for the widows who apparently were not given a fair shake in the distribution of food, they could give a straightforward assignment. It went something like this: find seven men who have a good track record. As big as the church was, they knew the track record of each individual. They were to find men of good reputation. They were to seek out people who demonstrated the control by the Spirit. And then what? They were to look for wisdom—one of the spiritual gifts. Why did they single out wisdom? Because wisdom is the particular ability of applying knowledge to its practical end. They would need that ability to solve the problem in the early church. The church leaders therefore went out looking for that kind of person. They knew the people, and they understood spiritual gifts and how to identify them.

In fact, one man in the early church demonstrated his spiritual gift so well that they named him by it: Joseph, who was nicknamed Barnabas (Acts 4:36). What does "Barnabas" mean? It means "Son of exhortation." Exhortation is the ability to come alongside another person, usually on a one-to-one level, and say things from the Word of God that lift that person up onto higher ground in Christ Jesus. So well did Barnabas practice his gift that they nicknamed him by it.

Would it not be phenomenal in mobilizing the church if we could refer to its members as "son of preaching," "son of teaching," "son of exhortation," "daughter of mercy," "daughter of helps," or whatever else, and be able to identify who they are? It surely would. Why? Because I cannot make my contribution to the unity of the church, as expounded in Ephesians 4:1-6, until I first understand my own identity. Who am I? What has God put in me? And how will I use what I am to contribute distinctively to the unity of the body of Christ? Unless I understand my own identity, I will not contribute to the unity of the church. This is why Romans 12:3-8 follows hard on the heels of the great exhortation in Romans 12:1-2. Unfortunately, most people have memorized the first two verses out of context, and they have thus ignored the important doctrine of spiritual gifting in the six verses that follow. Yet Paul urged believers "to think so as to have sound judgment, as God has allotted to each a measure of faith" (Romans 12:3). He went on to say that Christ gave gifts to each one of us.

As a result of the recent spate of material on spiritual gifts, I find the pendulum swinging again. Some are reacting to that and saying, "What I am really interested in is not your spiritual gifts but your maturity in Christ. What I am interested in is your attitude."

I am interested in their attitudes too; but I am also interested in their gifts. Let me give you an example. I am in the process of building a home. We have a contractor and a number of subcontractors. When that contractor comes with his tools—a plane and a hammer and a saw and all those other tools in a box—I want him to know what those tools are and how they are meant to be used. Now, I hope that when he uses them, he will have a good attitude. I hope he will be mature in his relationship with other subcontractors on the job. For example, we have one electrician who is a bummer. He has a bad mouth and a bad attitude. Most of the subcontractors are very good ones. They are amiable. They are easy to get along with. But not the electrician. Yet I would rather have the electrician I have, who knows what he is doing and does not have too good an attitude, than to have one with a very sweet attitude who did not know the difference between red, black, and white wires.

We do not need new encouragement for ignorance in the church. I like a statement that recently came out of Harvard: "If you think education is expensive, try ignorance." In a former generation, a man came up to John Wesley and said, "Mr. Wesley, I have been praying, and. God has told me that I ought to tell you that He does not need all of your Hebrew and all of your Greek and all of your learnin'."

Mr. Wesley responded, "Sir, I have not had the opportunity to pray about this; but before you ever told me that, I knew that God did not need my Hebrew and my Greek and all my learnin'. But may I suggest to you that God does not need all of your ignorance either." No, we do not need more ignorance today.

We do not need gifts *or* fruit; we need gifts *and* fruit. We need to know *who* we are; and then we need to use *what* we are. We need to use our gifts maturely, so that as we demonstrate them, people will see Jesus Christ in us and have their appetites whetted to know Him, whom to know is life everlasting. That is the desire of the Spirit of God as He seeks to implement the gifts of God through the body of Christ.

OUR LEADERS

One last area for investigation appears in Ephesians 4:11. We have seen that Christ not only gives vocation or calling; He also bestows gifts for carrying out the calling. Third, He takes out of the church certain ones and gives them a fulltime (for lack of a better term) function in their calling as a service to the rest of the body of Christ.

If you want to follow through the parallel with Israel, go back to Numbers 18 and see how God did it with them.

> *And behold, I Myself have taken your fellow Levites from among the sons of Israel; they are a gift to you, dedicated to the Lord, to perform the service for the tent of meeting*
>
> *~Numbers 18:6*

Everybody had something to do. Certain people were taken out from among the others and given back to them so that they could aid them in developing their spiritual gifts, so to speak. They would help them develop the tasks they were given to do, and lead them in doing them excellently.

The Provider of the Gifts

Thus in the church, God's new mediatorial people, "He gave some as apostles, and some as prophets, and some as evangelists, and some as pastors and teachers, for the equipping of the saints for the work of service, to the building up of the body of Christ" (Ephesians 4:11-12). The apostles and prophets, Paul said in Ephesians 2, were the foundation stones. Jesus Christ Himself shaped those stones, which were going to be put into place on the Day of Pentecost. Christ Himself was the Chief Cornerstone, from which all the lines of the building would be aligned and squared. He would be the focal point that would give direction to the building. So He shaped those foundation stones, the apostles and prophets (see Ephesians 2:20). Then He left it to the evangelists, pastors, and teachers to lead in a program of upbuilding, of shaping the living stones until the completion of the body. Then this body would be presented without fault, without distortion, a holy temple unto the Lord.

In conclusion, concerning God's provisions, let me suggest to you this thought: in those last three functions of evangelist, pastor, and teacher, a recent development has taken place. Some Bible scholars have put a hyphen between the last two and made it one gift. In addition, many churches have eliminated the evangelist from the local church staff. By so doing, they have effectively gotten the three separate functions down to a single jack-of-all-trades task. The one man who does them has undoubtedly been given the idea that he is the fourth member of the trinity—that he can be everywhere, that he knows all things, and that he can do all things.

God said there are three functions. I believe, on a solid grammatical basis, that there should *not* be a hyphen between "pastor" and "teacher." Rather, I would simply suggest that evangelist, pastor, and teacher are three separate functions in leadership for the erecting of the superstructure of the church. It is laid upon the foundation, and it is for the building up of the body of Christ—the shaping of the living stones to the doing of the ministry.

Why not look at your own local churches? Look at the leadership. Is it multiple? Is it filling those three functions—evangelist, pastor, and teacher? Do the people understand their spiritual gifts? Are they using their gifts in and through a specific area in your local church?

If they are not, then let me suggest a worthy goal for any church to take as its project. Determine to see that every member of that church knows who he is by reason of gifts, and that he is using those gifts to the glory of God and the fulfilling of the Great Commission that the ascended Head, Jesus Christ, gave to him. May God enable us to carry out that commission.

5

THE POSSESSOR OF THE BODY MEMBER

Let us review once more what we have already learned. We started the book with a look at Ephesians 5:1, "Be imitators of God." I suggested to you that your life will never be lived any higher than your understanding of God. The devil's greatest desire is to destroy our right concepts of God. If I really want to win in the battle for truth, therefore, I need to think right. And I need to begin by thinking right about what God is like. That is why the wise king in Proverbs taught us that the fear of the Lord is the beginning of knowledge. In these chapters, we have limited ourselves to a specific area of truth about God, and only part of that; namely, the truth about God the Holy Spirit and His relationship to God's children.

We started by considering God the Holy Spirit as the *pattern of dependency*. He demonstrates to us the kind of lifestyle we need to have. The Spirit of God is dependent upon God the Father and God the Son. And in this He gives us a pattern.

We moved from the Spirit as the pattern of dependency to the Spirit as our *power for witnessing*. The Spirit of truth serves as a defense attorney through God's children to make a case for Jesus Christ in the world.

We-moved from that to the Spirit of God as the *protector of the church* by His presence in us and among us. After the ascension of Jesus Christ to His place of headship at the right hand of the Father, He brought together Jew and Gentile in one new body called the "church." He then placed that body in the Spirit for care and safekeeping.

We moved from the Spirit of God as our protector to the Spirit of God as *our provider*. He accepts the assignments of the Son of God, the Head of the church, with respect to spiritual gifts. He distributes to every member of the body a specific gift or gifts for use in a specific vocation or calling in and through the particular local church to which that believer belongs.

In this chapter we come back to the passage where we started, Ephesians 5, where we learn about *the Spirit of God as our possessor*. The text used most frequently as the central passage for revealing this aspect of the Spirit's work is Ephesians 5:18. This teaching is referred to under the designation, "the filling of the Spirit."

FILLING OF THE SPIRIT

I believe that the Word of God refers to our life in God in numerous ways. It is like a huge, multifaceted diamond that has multitudinous reflections, depending upon the direction of the light on the facets. Sometimes when the Word of God refers to that life, it talks about it as "abiding in Christ." Other times it refers to it as "being filled in the Spirit." Still other times it is spoken of as "walking in the Spirit," or "not grieving the Spirit." Those are not references to different kinds of living. They refer to the same kind of living, but they are being looked at from slightly different perspectives.

I am a little bothered by the practice of taking a specific word or phrase or verse of Scripture and making it the standard by which we interpret everything else in the Bible. Altogether too often, the phrase "the filling of the Spirit" has become just that. It has become a magical *cliché* from which we launch a theology that is not founded upon a broad base in the Scriptures, but is based upon the experiences people gather out of life.

The central passage is Ephesians 5:18, "And do not get drunk with wine, for that is dissipation, but be filled with the Spirit."

But if we look back at Ephesians 4, we see references to a word that is used far more frequently than "filling," and that is the word "walk." But we do not have as great a doctrine developed today on the *walk* in the Spirit as we do on the *filling* of the Spirit. In Ephesians 4:1 we read, "I, therefore, the prisoner of the Lord, entreat you to walk in a manner worthy of the calling"—a worthy walk. Ephesians 4:17 says, "This I say therefore, and affirm together with the Lord, that you walk no longer just as the Gentiles also walk, in the futility of their mind." We're not to have this kind of negative walk. Moving on to Ephesians 5:2, Paul wrote, "[As an imitator of God] walk in love." Then in Ephesians 5:8, we read, "Walk as children of light." Finally, down in Ephesians 5:15, Paul writes "Therefore be careful how you walk."

It would seem to me that if one word is emphasized in these chapters, it is the word "walk." The passage is talking about a step-by-step, moment-by-moment walk. If we allow the context to explain what Paul means by being filled with the Spirit, he describes it as walking with the Spirit.

Let us take another approach. Paul authored more than one book from that prison cell in Rome. In fact, he wrote more than one book on the church at that time. He sent letters about the church to the Ephesians, and to the Colossians as well. The book of Ephesians places primary emphasis on the body of which Jesus Christ is the Head; however, Colossians places the emphasis primarily on Christ, the Head, of which we are the members of His body. Consequently, we should expect to see many similarities between Ephesians and Colossians.

The teaching of Paul's letter to Ephesus was intended to counter some of the heresies they were facing in that city—especially with respect to the goddess Diana of the Ephesians and some of the mystery religions. When Paul wrote to Colossae, he wrote primarily about the same truth. But he oriented it around the kinds of heresies that were plaguing the Colossian church and denigrating the name of Christ. The apostle lifted Christ up in their midst and said that He is to have first place in all things. The Gnostic heresy of Colossae needed to be attacked by a different approach than did the mystery religions of Ephesus. But the underlying truth is much the same. So, when we read those books, we see similar subject matter with a little different orientation.

To get that in mind, keep your finger in Ephesians 5 and turn to Colossians 3. Here we will observe one comparison that illustrates the point. First, read the whole paragraph that begins with Ephesians 5:15. Paul said,

> *Therefore be careful how you walk, not as unwise men, but as wise, making the most of your time, because the days are evil. So then do not be foolish, but understand* [be mentally perceiving] *what the will of the Lord is.*
>
> *~Ephesians 5:15-17*

I interject that Paul did not say, "Be feeling the will of the Lord," even though that is the way we usually talk about it. Rather, he told us to be mentally perceiving what the will of the Lord is. The passage continues,

> *And do not get drunk with wine, for that is dissipation, but be filled with the Spirit, speaking to one another in psalms and hymns and spiritual songs, singing and making melody with your heart to the Lord; always giving thanks for all things in the name of our Lord Jesus Christ to God, even the Father; and be subject to one another in the fear of Christ.*
>
> *~Ephesians 5:18-21*

With that in mind, now read Colossians 3:15 and following:

> *And let the peace of Christ rule in your hearts, to which indeed you were called in one body; and be*

thankful. Let the word of Christ richly dwell within you [or, let the word of Christ settle down in you richly], *with all wisdom teaching and admonishing one another with psalms and hymns and spiritual songs, singing with thankfulness in your hearts to God. And whatever you do in word or deed, do all in the name of the Lord Jesus, giving thanks through Him to God the Father.*
~ Colossians 3:15-17

Notice that the content in Ephesians 5 and in Colossians 3 is substantially the same—except for the introductory statement. The statement in Ephesians is, "Be filled with the Spirit." In the Colossian letter, his statement is, "Let the word of Christ [settle down in you] richly." Paul approached from two different standpoints because of the two different heresies about Christ he was counteracting in their respective cities—the mysticism of Ephesus as opposed to the Gnosticism of Colossae. He put those two in proper perspective. But he was really not talking about two different kinds of living; rather, he was talking about one lifestyle that will glorify God.

In mathematics class we learn that things that equal the same thing are equal to each other. Here you have two things that equal the same thing: being filled with the Spirit brings the same result as letting the word of Christ settle down in you richly. What may I learn from that? I think I may learn that it is impossible to be filled with the Spirit apart from letting the word of Christ settle down in me richly. Or vice versa. It is impossible to let the word of Christ settle down in me richly apart from being controlled by the Spirit.

Earlier in the book, I suggested that the Spirit of God is mute apart from the Word of God. The Spirit speaks through the Word. Without the Word, He has nothing to say. So also, the Word of God apart from the Spirit of God is lifeless—it is without power to act. The Word of God approached apart from the Spirit of God will lead to fanaticism. But when the Spirit of God is vitally conjoined with the truths of the Word of God, it spells victory in the believer's life. We therefore can learn something about the filling work of the Spirit of God simply by letting our eyes look a little further in the context of the book of Ephesians, and then by looking in a parallel volume, Colossians. Thus we are guided by the whole of biblical teaching.

THE FILLING EXPLAINED

Look more closely at the phrase in Ephesians 5:18, "Be filled with the Spirit." The apostle is obviously making a contrast here between being controlled by wine, which leads to excess, and being controlled by the Spirit. The Greek word translated "fill" was used to refer to both material things and nonmaterial things. When it was used to refer to material things, one could translate it by the English word we are familiar with—the word "filling," which means to fill something up. Unfortunately, people have used that idea with regard to the Spirit of God, who is nonmaterial. I have often heard illustrations like this: If I have a glass and a pitcher of water, I can fill that glass half full or two-thirds full or three-fourths full. Then the person will say, "That is like the filling of the Spirit."

What to Expect from the Holy Spirit

I know nothing more *unlike* the filling of the Spirit! The Spirit is nonmaterial; He is spirit. And you do not fill up materially with the spiritual. The Spirit is not an "it," even though we often mistakenly refer to Him as an "it." He is a "he," not an "it." He is a person. And you do not get pieces of persons. You do not get little bits of the Holy Spirit as you move along. You do not get more and more of the Spirit. He does not come that way.

That is why Paul said so clearly, "If anyone does not hear the Spirit of Christ, he does not belong to Him" (Romans 8:9). The dear soul who claims to be a believer but is still praying for the reception of the Spirit is either not in Christ or is ignorant of what Paul was saying in Romans 8.

You do not get the Spirit piece-by-piece any more than when a man and woman go to the altar and take each other, they receive an arm of each other or a leg of each other, and later on some more of each other. At the "marriage" between Christ and the believer, he receives the Spirit. He not only receives the Spirit, he receives God—Father, Son, and Holy Spirit—at that monumental moment of transaction. As he lives out the Christian life, he progressively understands what he possesses. And the more he understands of God and what He is doing in his life, the more he lives out that which he understands.

"Filling" may be a good rendering of the Greek term here when you are speaking of material things, but it is not a good rendering when you are speaking of the abstract, or of a person such as the Holy Spirit. We have seen other words used; namely, "possess" or "control." When we are talking about abstract things or persons like the Spirit, it is far easier to understand if we say, "being controlled by the Spirit" or "being possessed by the Spirit" than if we say, "being filled by the Spirit."

That which possesses or controls produces its own product. In the New Testament, therefore, the person who is filled with sorrow is possessed with sorrow, and he produces the results of it. The person who is filled with fear is possessed with fear, and he produces the results of it. The person who is filled with joy is possessed by joy, and he produces the results of it. I will always have the result of that which possesses me. In the nontheological area, the word translated "filled" was used of a wind that could fill the sail of a ship. Having filled the sail, it would move it. It would control it. It would possess it.

Consequently, that which fills me is that which possesses or controls me. At every moment in my life, I am submitting myself to one of two possible controls. I have the potential of dual control, but not both at the same time. You may drive a dual-control car up to a corner and turn left or right, but you could not turn both ways at the same time—even though there are two controls. In my life, as a result of my new birth, I now have the potential of a new control.

Before I came to Jesus Christ, I continually did the will of the devil. I was enslaved to him. Even the best acts I did—even the most benevolent, altruistic things I did—were sin in God's sight, because they were not done and could not be done to the glory of God. They were done outside of submission to Jesus Christ. No act, no matter how good, done outside of submission to Jesus Christ is anything but sin in God's sight. Before I came to Jesus Christ, therefore, everything that I did was only evil continually.

When I came to Christ, the tyranny of Satan was broken. Scripture teaches me this in Romans 6 and numerous other passages. The devil's right to rule was gone. I now had the potential of submitting my life, moment by moment, to God rather than the devil for control. And I am working to do precisely that, moment by moment by moment.

A REPEATED ACT

When you study Ephesians 5:18, note that the word translated "filled" is in the present tense. It speaks of something that happens moment by moment by moment. It is being repeated continuously. If you want to get very technical, this word is an iterative present. It is not simply a durative, something that goes on and flows smoothly, but it is something that happens repeatedly.

The control happens as repeatedly as the thoughts you have. Every thought that comes into your mind is an opportunity for control. That is why Paul was so meticulous in 2 Corinthians 10 when he told us to bring "every thought captive to the obedience of Christ" (2 Corinthians 10:5). Do not let one thought run loose. Why? Because thoughts are the raw materials of actions. If I entertain a thought and dwell on it, and it is not a thought that will ultimately produce good action, then it will produce sin. It will not bring glory to God. In James 1:13-15 is given the evolution of a thought into a sin and consequently into death; that is,

The Possessor of the Body Member

separation. Every thought I have, then, is an opportunity for control. I would suggest to you that if you and I had the ability to isolate every thought and to line them all up, as Jesus Christ has the ability to do, we would find that every thought we have, when evaluated according to the motivation behind it, will fall either on the side of God or on the side of the devil. Yes, it is important how we think!

So the apostle said that this filling, this possession, this control of the Spirit is a moment-by-moment-by-moment-by-moment process. I emphasize that because some people get into a situation where they say, "Let us all pray now, and let us pray to be filled with the Spirit." The dear person with utter sincerity prays, "God, fill me." Then the prayer is over and he supposedly is filled. One feels like saying, "Do not bump me. You might knock it out of me because now I am filled."

Filled with respect to what? There can be no such bland filling. Filling must always have an object. Possession (or control) must always have an object. And that object must always be the Word of God. Consequently, suppose I am reading the passage that says, "Husbands, love your wives," and it tells me to nourish and cherish her. Then my wife calls me on the phone and says, "Honey, I tell you, this has got to stop. You have got to stop running back to Chicago and New York and all these places. And you have got to stay home. I want to tell you, I am going out of my mind." Then I say, "Hey, why don't you get off my back? Don't you know I am serving God?" Then I go back and have my devotions, and the Word says, "Husbands, love your wives." Nourish her. Cherish her. God the Holy Spirit takes that Word, and He drives it right into me. He sticks the sword in under the third rib and says, "How about that?" He is not going to let me loose from it until I get back on the phone and say, "Honey, I am sorry. I was unthinking. Would you please forgive me? I will endeavor to stay home more." That is the meaning of control by the Spirit.

To be filled, to be controlled, to be possessed in Spirit must have relation to an object. And that object is always the Word of God. Being filled with the Spirit is not just reaching some kind of plateau. It is not some kind of state that I reach, never to be repeated again. It is not a feeling. It is not tingles, shivers, and goose bumps. It is a moment-by-moment encounter between myself and the Word of truth by the Spirit of God. Every thought provides a new opportunity for control.

Interestingly, the same word "filled," used in Ephesians 5:18 with reference to the Spirit, is used in Acts 5:3 with reference to Satan. When I agree with the Word, and when I do what the Word says in that specific act, I am being controlled and possessed by the Spirit of God. But when I go contrary to the Word, I am being possessed by, controlled by, the devil.

The more I repeatedly submit my thoughts to God for control, the more obvious becomes the manifestation of the fruit of the Spirit in my life, and the faster I will move into maturity in Jesus Christ. There is no metaphysical hocus-pocus about this. It is not mysterious. It is a moment-by-moment control of the thoughts that enter into my life. I do something with every thought.

The Possessor of the Body Member

APPLICATION

Paul said in Ephesians 5:19 that if I am being controlled by the Spirit moment by moment, I will first of all have *rejoicing in song* pouring forth out of my heart. Why? Because I know that singing is one simple thing I can do that is God's opportunity to bring glory to Himself. The person who does not sing in the light of Ephesians 5:19—"speaking to one another in psalms and hymns and spiritual songs, singing and making melody with your heart to the Lord"—is missing one of the finest opportunities to glorify God. Paul writes about three types of singing: Psalms, hymns, and spiritual songs. Some people never get out of the psalter. They ought to learn some songs. Some never learn anything but songs. They ought to get into the psalter. There ought to be a grand diversity in our expression of intelligent praise to God. And there will be, if we are controlled in Spirit.

Second, I will be *giving thanks always for all things* through Jesus Christ to God my Father. As a seminary professor, I often noticed that after we have gotten the semester going for a few days and the students begin to get their assignments, they get a little different attitude than they had for the first few days. They come dreaming of just sitting under those biblical scholars who are going to pour out all of those goodies from the Word of God, and they want to catch it all. Then all of a sudden they begin to get assignments. They begin to find out how "ivory tower" their professors really are. The student thinks: "They do not have any sense at all. Any one of them gives us more work than one person could possibly do for all courses all year long." The old carnal nature begins to rise up. They begin griping to one another. Then I come along with a message, and I say, "I want to help you. You are going to find people that come around griping to you. So, to help those people, simply ask them, 'When did you get out of the control of the Spirit of God? And how could I help you to get back in?'" It is as simple as that. If a person is walking around griping, by whom is he controlled? The devil. Not God. He is playing on the devil's team at that point.

The university I attended had a good slogan: "Constructive suggestions appreciated; griping not tolerated." The easiest way to get shipped from that school was griping. I like that, because if I am really walking in tune with the Spirit of God, there will be a very practical result. I will be giving thanks always to God the Father in the name of our Lord Jesus Christ. There are proper channels through which to funnel constructive suggestions. Griping is never of God. Giving thanks is.

Third, Paul said that we will be *submitting ourselves one to another* in the fear of God. I think the highest, most beautiful display of the life of the Spirit of God in a believer is seen in mutual dependency—in a spirit of submission. Anyone can rebel. It doesn't take any spiritual qualifications to be a rebel. But to be in submission takes strength, because we do not naturally bend our wills to the will of another.

In this passage Paul is teaching us domestic submission in the home and at the job. In Romans 13, he gives us civil submission with regard to the government. And in Hebrews 13, he gives us ecclesiastical submission with regard to the church. All the way through is this beautiful attitude of the Spirit-controlled believer. He is one who is in submission. Some people think that is weakness; however, I think it is spiritual strength. I remember a statement given by Guy King in one of his helpful little commentaries: "If you think meekness is weakness, then just try being meek for a week."

If we are really interested in honoring the Spirit of God, we will honor the Word of God, which honors the Son of God, whose very desire is to do the will of God the Father. I close by saying again, as I did at the beginning, "Be imitators of God" (Ephesians 5:1). It is God who provides both the inner motivation for, and the outward expression of, a person's spiritual gift.

CONCLUSION

By Jeremy Myers

[Publisher's Note: This conclusion was not in the original edition of the book. Since the original 1983 edition of this book consisted of the transcriptions of several messages that Dr. Earl Radmacher had given on the topic of the Holy Spirit, the publishers felt that a brief concluding chapter was needed to summarize and wrap up the ideas and themes of the earlier chapters. This chapter is drawn from an article Jeremy Myers wrote for TillHeComes.org.]

Now we have come to the end of the book. Yet despite all the excellent and biblical information in this book, you may be asking yourself, "Yes, but I'm still not sure I fully understand how the Holy Spirit works or how to make Him work through my life."

Is this how you feel? Good. This is the way God wants it. When it comes to working with God, you should never feel like you are in control of Him. You should never get to the place where you think you know all there is to know about Him. This is especially true of the Holy Spirit.

A lot of theology tries to hold on to God, box Him up, tie Him down. We try to corner Him, and make sure there are no loose ends. But if we are honest with ourselves, we discover that the more we try to make God fit into our definitions and explanations of Him, the more He slips from our grasps and eludes our understanding. Once again, this is especially true of the Holy Spirit.

The more we chase Him, the faster He runs. The more we try to trap Him, the less we see of Him. God's tricky that way.

It's like trying to catch a fish with your bare hands. Have you ever tried it? The more you move, the further away they swim.

Or if not a fish, have you ever chased a duck around a yard? A goat in a field? A cat down a street? They don't want to be caught, and the more you run, the further away they get.

God is like that. Especially the Holy Spirit. Maybe that is why an old Celtic title for the Holy Spirit is the Wild Goose. He doesn't like to be chased. He doesn't like to be cornered. He is elusive. Unruly. Wild.

Free.

And yet, the Bible tells us over and over that God loves to be near us. He wants to be found. The Spirit, like a dove descending upon Jesus, seeks to descend into our life and commune with us, share life with us, and lead us into all truth. How does this happen?

Though you cannot chase after a fish, a duck, or a goat and catch one (most of the time), you can get

Conclusion

them to come to you. How? By being still. Moving slow. And offering something they want.

I recently had a fish swim right through my hands. I might even have been able to pull one out of the water if I wanted. How did this happen? I laid down on a dock which had fish swimming beneath it. I then slowly and gently put my hands down into the water. Finally, I had my wife sprinkle a handful of breadcrumbs into the water around where the fish were swimming. You know what happened next. Rather than swimming away from me, they swam toward me. In fact, they swarmed me. I felt them swimming through my hands, darting at the bread crumbs which swirled through the water. Under the right circumstances, the fish came to me.

The same thing also works for ducks, goats, and even cats. We can sit still. Be quiet. Offer them something they want. Then, when they are ready, they will come to you, without you having to take a step.

The Holy Spirit, of course, is not a fish, a duck, a goat, or a cat. Nevertheless, we can learn about God from creation (Romans 1), and even the Scriptures occasionally teach us about God by using animal imagery. So when we think about the Holy Spirit, it is helpful to remember that like the fish or the wild goose, He cannot be trapped or cornered. Instead, like the wind, He moves where He will (John 3:8). But if we sit back, resting in the presence of God and the knowledge of His Word, we know that the Spirit will come to us, fill us with His power, and move us to love and serve others in the name of Jesus.

Which brings up one final point. One of the goals of the Holy Spirit is to bring glory to Jesus Christ. Jesus said that the Spirit, when He comes, will testify about Him, that is, Jesus (John 14:26). The Spirit does not glorify Himself, but lifts up the name of Jesus and points people to Him.

I think sometimes the Spirit gets embarrassed by all the attention He receives in some churches today. He is the still, small voice. He is heard only in the quiet. He descends like a dove, which is a symbol for peace. The Spirit likes to be in the background. He likes to stay in the wings, off stage. When the Spirit is at work, He lifts up the name of Jesus. When people are filled with the Spirit, He rarely inspires them to talk about Himself, but to talk about Jesus and glorify His Name.

Do you want to understand the Spirit more? Do you want to be filled with the Spirit and see Him at work in your life? I hope so. He wants this too. But rather than work yourself into a frenzy trying to make yourself look "spiritual," just sit back, be still, and let Him know through prayer that you are available. By faith, know that you have been indwelled, baptized, and sealed by the Spirit of God. Then, going forth in faith, look for ways that the Holy Spirit might want to lift up the name of Jesus, build up the Body of Christ, and advancing the message of the gospel in the world. As you do this, know that the Holy Spirit will be at work in your life, for these are the things that can only be done by the power of the Spirit.

APPENDIX

By Dr. Stephen R. Lewis
President, Rocky Mountain Bible College & Seminary

[Publisher's Note: The following appendix was not in the original edition of this book, but has been added as a supplement to summarize the theology of the Holy Spirit in relation to the church.]

And I will ask the Father, and He will give you another Helper, that He may be with you forever; that is the Spirit of truth, whom the world cannot receive, because it does not behold Him or know Him, but you know Him because He abides with you forever.
-John 14:16-17

These words from the Lord Jesus raised the expectations of His discouraged disciples. Something new and wonderful was about to happen. In just a few days, when the Spirit would come, He would live inside them. Unlike their Master who was about to leave them, the Spirit's presence would be permanent. This had never happened before. Note even with the greatest leaders of the Old Testament.

Sadly, today many believers are confused by the ministry of the Spirit in their lives. The religious lingo seems so unfamiliar—indwelling, sealing, baptism, gifting, filling. How do you know if any of these have happened? When should I expect it? How will I know?

Dividing the ministries of the Holy Spirit into three primary categories helps us appreciate their importance in our Christian experience. In relation to *eternal life*, the Holy Spirit provides indwelling and sealing. In relation to *everyday life*, the Holy Spirit providing filling and living. In relation to *body life*, the Holy Spirit provides baptizing and gifting.

At the heart of these ministries lies the work of the Spirit in the divine transaction which initiates and guarantees eternal life to all who believe in the Lord Jesus.

INDWELLING AND SEALING

At the heart of the biblical teaching on the Holy Spirit's indwelling and sealing is the truth that each believer has all the Holy Spirit they will ever get. This truth is seen when we understand what the Bible has to say about the indwelling and sealing work of the Holy Spirit.

When people believe in Jesus Christ, God's Spirit indwells and seals them forever. Paul writes in Romans 8:9 that the Holy Spirit permanently indwells every Christian the moment they believe. There is no delay between believing in Jesus for eternal life and receiving the Spirit of God. Once a person believes in Jesus, they are indwelt by the Spirit. Just like eternal life, the indwelling Spirit is a gift from God to all believers (John 7:37; Acts 11:16-17; Romans 5:5; 1 Corinthians 2:12; 2 Corinthians 5:5).

The fact that the indwelling Spirit is gift of God is reinforced by the biblical teaching that even sinning believers are indwelled by the Spirit (1 Corinthians 5:5; 6:1ff). Though some believe that the Holy Spirit abandons believers when they sin, this is not what Scripture teaches. The Holy Spirit indwells believers forever (John 14:16).

The indwelling of the Spirit is closely related to the sealing of the Spirit. The Holy Spirit permanently seals every believer the moment they believe (Ephesians 1:13). This sealing of the Holy Spirit is a permanent guarantees that they will receive all that God has promised (2 Corinthians 1:22). Just like the indwelling of the Spirit, the Spirit's sealing is simultaneous to belief (Ephesians 1:13), and even sinning believers remain sealed by the Holy Spirit (2 Corinthians 1:22; Ephesians 4:30). This means that the sealing of the Holy Spirit cannot be lost. The Spirit seals believers until the day of redemption (Ephesians 4:30).

These truths provide great encouragement for the believer. The Spirit's indwelling and sealing ministries bring security and purity to our Christian experience.

The fact that the Holy Spirit permanently indwells and seals every believer means that we have all the Holy Spirit we will ever get. We are secure in our relationship with God. The Spirit cannot leave believers (Romans 8:9), and will indwell every believer forever (John 14:16). Though sin affects the *effectiveness* of the Spirit in the Christian's life, sin does not remove the *presence* of the Spirit from their life.

In this way, the sealing of the Spirit is a great comfort to Christians. The sealing by the Holy Spirit includes the ideas of ownership, authority, and responsibility. Therefore, sealing assures believers of the security of God's promises, especially the promise of salvation. The Bible teaches that sealing is to the day of redemption which will culminate with the reception of resurrected bodies (Romans 8:23). Notice that the sealing it is to the day of redemption, not to the day of sinning or failure. Sealing is permanent!

Such a teaching, of course, does not lead a person into being free to sin all they want, but rather, is an encouragement to remain pure in their daily conduct. The sealing of the Spirit encourages us to remain pure. This occurs in at least two ways.

First, the Spirit's indwelling makes our body the "temple of the Holy Spirit" bought with a price (1 Corinthians 6:19). We want to keep God's blood-bought "house" clean!

Second, the Spirit's sealing marks us as God's property. Since God owns our minds and bodies, He has an invested interest in keeping His property pure, and we, as the "tenants" in His property, want to please our Landlord and Helper rather than grieve Him (Ephesians 4:30).

How then can you know that you have received the Holy Spirit? There is only one way to receive the Holy Spirit: You must be born again with life from above. The Lord Jesus promises to give His life, eternal life to anyone who believes in Him. This new life is empowered by the Spirit. So it's a package deal. If you want the power to live a new life, you must first receive a new life to start with. Christ died for sin and arose. Believe in Jesus Christ today and He will give you everlasting life and power to live that life abundantly through His Spirit (John 6:47; 10:10).

FILLING AND LIVING

The filling of the Spirit is different than being indwelled by the Spirit. While the indwelling and sealing of the Spirit is instantaneous and permanent to all who believe in Jesus, the filling of the Spirit and living by the Spirit depends upon the ongoing trust and yielding of the believer. Though all believers have the indwelling Spirit, not all believers are filled, or controlled, by the Spirit (Ephesians 5:18). When you have trusted God enough to relinquish control of your life to the Spirit, you are filled!

The filling of the Holy Spirit seems to be of two different types. The first type of filling is more general in nature and character and is available to all believers. In this filling, the Spirit has extensive influence and control in a believer's life. Scripture commands every believer to be filled with the Spirit in this way (Ephesians 5:18), and it occurs when the overall character of a person is controlled by the Spirit (Acts 6:3; 13:52).

There is a second type of filling however, which seems to be more specialized in nature and focus. Sometimes, the filling of the Spirit is a sovereign work of God providing special enablement for specific times (Exodus 35:31; Acts 2:4; 4:8, 31; 13:9; Luke 1:67). In this special type of Spirit-filling, God possesses someone for special activity (Luke 1:15—John the Baptist; Luke 1:41—Elizabeth; Luke 1:67—Zacharias; Acts 2:4—the group the Day of Pentecost; Acts 4:8—Peter; Acts 4:31—the believers; Acts 9:17—Paul; Acts 13:9—Paul). The Bible does not say much about this filling except that it happens. Some feel we should not ask for this type of filling, while others feel comfortable asking for this special filling.

Some of tried to equate the work of the Spirit in the church age with the work of the Spirit prior to Pentecost, but Scripture indicates that the Spirit's filling is unique among His ministries in the church age since it requires Christians to yield to His control. This truth is seen in numerous ways.

First, the command in Ephesians 5:18 to "be filled with the Spirit" is the present, passive, plural, imperative (Gk., *plērousthe*), meaning "to pervade with an influence, to dominate or control behavior." To emphasize the imperative, it could be translated, "You be filled!" This is a command; it needs a response. The comparison Paul makes is with getting drunk with wine. Just as a drunk chooses to give control of his or her life to alcohol, believers must choose to give control of their life to God's Spirit.

The contrast with the Holy Spirit's other ministries tells us that opening our lives to the filling of the Holy Spirit is the personal responsibility of every believer. While the indwelling, sealing, and baptizing work of the Holy Spirit occurs only once in each believer's life, never happened before the day of Pentecost, is true of all believers, results in position and potential, occurs instantaneously upon faith in Jesus, and has no prerequisite except faith, the filling of the Spirit is a repeatable process, did occur in the Old Testament, is not necessarily experienced by all, results in power for service, occurs throughout the Christian life, and depends upon trust and yieldedness to the Spirit of God.

So how can believers be filled with the Holy Spirit? We must simply trust and yield to Him. We must trust God enough to give the Holy Spirit control of our life (Ephesians 5:18). When we do this, the filling of the Holy Spirit unleashes God's power into our life, so that we can be sanctified according to the image of Christ, and serve God with power and holiness as He desires and intends.

Yet while the issue is control, the conflict is inner. This inner conflict leads to the right way of living for God. To be filled with the Spirit is to be controlled by the Spirit (Ephesians 5:18), but our flesh fights the Spirit for control of our life. The flesh is the capacity to live life independently of God. Its disposition is to sin and oppose God (Romans 7:18; 1 Corinthians 3:3; 2 Corinthians 1:12; Galatians 5:17; Colossians 2:18; 2 Peter 2:10; 1 John 2:16). Like the Spirit, the flesh produces works (Galatians 5:19). Unlike the Spirit, these works never produce righteousness (Romans 7:18) and will eventually enslave the believer (Romans 7:25). You can never get rid of the flesh on earth, but you can overcome the flesh by walking in the Spirit. That is living in a Spirit-filled state—in dependence on the Holy Spirit, under His control rather than depending on your own strength (Galatians 5:16)

When we are filled with the Spirit and walk in the Spirit, we will not act like my without-Christ self. We will be a joyously worshiping, thankful, and cooperative member of the church (Ephesians 5:18-21). We will be more like Christ as the Spirit displays His fruit through our yielded life (Galatians 5:22-23). We will bless those around us. The Holy Spirit overflows in the life of Spirit-filled believers, spreading the blessing they have received (John 7:37-39).

Many Christians try to live their lives on their own power and wisdom, without the filling of the Holy Spirit. This is partly why many Christians live such defeated and empty lives. We need to be filled with the Spirit because we can't do life on our own.

The issue isn't how much of the Holy Spirit we have or how much of the Holy Spirit's power we can get. Due to indwelling and sealing, we have all of the Spirit we are ever going to get. The issue for Christians is how much of us does the Holy Spirit have! He will take whatever we give Him and use it to glorify Christ (1 Corinthians 3:18).

Instead of trying to be out in front of our lives—manipulating God and others as we design our future, we realize that God is inside of us—moving us toward His design for our future.

BAPTIZING AND GIFTING

When it comes to body life, an understanding of the baptism and gifting of the Spirit is absolutely critical to experiencing the joy and confidence of living in community. The purpose of the Holy Spirit's ministries during the church age is to glorify Christ (John 16:14) by building His body—the church. When the Spirit indwells and seals us, he does not simply come to dwell with us, but also comes to empower us to glorify Christ

Appendix

by loving and serving Him and one another in the church. When people believe in Jesus, God's Spirit baptizes them into the body of Christ and provides gifts to each person so that they can love and serve others (1 Corinthians 12:13).

The baptism of the Spirit was first predicted by John the Baptist (Matthew 3:11). Jesus provided further details about this baptism just prior to His ascension. He said this baptism would occur "not many days from now" (Acts 1:5). This specific ministry of the Holy Spirit served one purpose, and it continues to serve this purpose today: the baptism of the Holy Spirit adds believers to the body of Christ. It incorporates new believers into Jesus Christ. The dramatic events of Pentecost recorded in Acts 2:1-13 included the initial baptism of the Spirit, with the filling and gifting of the Spirit occurring simultaneously. Peter would later call this the initial fulfillment of Jesus' prophecy that His followers would be "baptized with the Holy Spirit" (Acts 11:15-16).

The central text regarding the baptism of the Holy Spirit is 1 Corinthians 12:13, which clearly states that all (even the unfaithful Corinthians!) have been baptized by the Spirit. As such, this baptism takes place simultaneously with the indwelling of the Holy Spirit—"all made to drink of the one Spirit." The emphasis of the passage is the unity of believers, just as it is in Ephesians 4:5, which also refers to the "one baptism" of the Spirit that all believers share.

How then does Spirit baptism differ from indwelling and the other works of the Spirit? According to Charles Ryrie, "Spirit baptism is Christ's work through the agency of the ministry of the Holy Spirit to join those who believe to the church, the body of Christ, with all the privileges and responsibilities that come with that position."

It is important to note as well that nowhere in Scripture is there one exhortation to be baptized with the Spirit. In the seven places that refer to the baptism of the Spirit, no one is a command to be baptized. Five passages predict that it will happen (Matthew 3:11; Mark 1:8; Luke 3:16; John 1:33; Acts 1:5), one looks back to the time it happened the first time to describe its recurrence with new believers (Acts 11:16), and one simply states that it has happened to all believers in the context of an exhortation to unity (1 Corinthians 12:13).

Many who sincerely believe they have been "baptized with the Spirit" as a second work of grace are simply confusing the baptism of the Spirit with an experience of being filled with the Spirit (Ephesians 5:18). Water baptism, though an important step of obedience for every believer to identify with the body of Christ, is different from the supernatural ministry of the Spirit to baptize us into the body of Christ. Spirit baptism is not dependent upon water baptism, and the biblical teaching on these types of baptism must not be confused.

Along with the baptism of the Spirit, we are given gifts of the Spirit. The Holy Spirit gives gifts to every believer for service in the body of Christ—the church—the moment they believe (1 Peter 4:10). A spiritual gift is a God-given capacity to serve the body of Christ wherever and however He dictates.

The gifting of the Spirit is purpose-oriented rather than person-oriented. The gifts of the Spirit are distributed to believers for the express purpose of building up the body of Christ—the church (Romans 12:4; 1 Corinthians 12:7; 14:4-5; Ephesians 4:12). As such, thought believers receive gifts as a result of being baptized with the Spirit, the use of spiritual gifts is connected to being filled with the Spirit.

There are two lists of spiritual gifts in the New Testament: Romans 12 and 1 Corinthians 12. Since the lists differ from one another, they seem to be non-exhaustive catalogues of gifts the Spirit gives. The ascension gifts described in Ephesians 4:11 seem to be gifts of leaders especially empowered to build the church rather than gifts given to individual believers.

The Spirit's baptism and gifting gather us in redemptive communities to love and serve one another and our world in ways that glorify the Lord Jesus Christ. Believers have all the Spiritual power they will ever need to serve Christ in the local church, if they are willing to do what it takes to get along with their partners in the Gospel (Philippians 1:5-7). Experiencing the one baptism serves as the basis for and exhortation to keep the unity of the body (Ephesians 4:5). The diversity of gifts being distributed by God's sovereign will explains the need for and the plea for cooperation in the body (1 Corinthians 12).

It is therefore essential that believer remain willing to do what is necessary to exercise their gifts in the church (Romans 12:1-2). The Spirit's gifting of believers—like all of the ministries of the Spirit—is designed to glorify Christ, not Himself (John 16:14), and definitely not the individual believer. We have been given gifts to glorify Christ by serving Him in the local church (Ephesians 4:12). The only way to discover our giftedness is to use our giftedness in service (Romans 12:6).

If you desire to know what gifts the Spirit of God has given you, simply examine the Word, exercise and train your spiritual muscles through service, and expect God to use you powerfully in the local church. Through practice, experimentation, the encouragement from other believers, and the wise input from church leaders, you will come to discern how God has gifted you, and what role God wants you to play in the church.

ABOUT THE AUTHOR

Dr. Earl D. Radmacher was born over seventy years ago in Portland, Oregon just a couple miles from Western Seminary where, in the providence of God, he would later serve on the theological faculty for thirty-three years (1962-1995) and in administrative positions as Dean of the Faculty (1964-1965), President (1965-1990), and Chancellor (1990-1995). In 1995 he was designated President Emeritus and Distinguished Professor of Systematic Theology Emeritus.

His parents, who were immigrants from Romania and Austria, settled in Portland in 1913 where they brought eight children into this world, Earl being the last. The whole family was very active in local churches so every Sunday found Earl spending all day in church - Sunday school, morning worship, potluck lunch at the church, recreation break, youth service, evening service, and after service. Even though he had heard the gospel preached Sunday after Sunday, he did not personally receive Christ as his Savior until he was fourteen years of age. He has often stated that sitting in church Sunday after Sunday doesn't make one a Christian any more than sitting in a garage makes one a car.

At that juncture in his life, Earl came in contact with another Earl—Earl Gile—a faithful Sunday school teacher who lived right across the street from the grade school he had attended, and he opened up his home as an outreach to boys from the school. Mr. Gile's church rented the school gymnasium on Thursday nights and made it available for boys to play basketball if they came to Sunday School on Sundays. That sounded like a good deal, so he went. Shortly after that, the teacher announced a forthcoming boys camp at Twin Rocks Beach, Oregon. He decided to go; and there, at fourteen years of age, he accepted Christ as his Savior.

Although the church preached the gospel faithfully, they didn't go beyond the gospel to build up believers in the faith. He has often said, "As a believer, I didn't need a birth message, but I did need a growth message. That being absent, I tended to flounder, and my growth in Christ was stunted. Thus, the high school years were a disaster as far as the things of Christ and spiritual growth were concerned."

As graduation time neared, he took the normal batch of tests to determine which line of work he should pursue. The tests indicated mathematics or mechanics, so he decided to go the route of mathematics and join it with money by starting a career in a saving and loan institution. He started as a file clerk and worked up to an investment statistician that year.

His plans in the investment business were dramatically interrupted, however, by a visit to Portland of a new evangelist on the scene, Billy Graham, in August of 1950. A friend invited him to go to the meeting and,

About the Author

although he had little spiritual appetite at the time, God seemed to press him toward the affirmative. As the poet Francis Thompson has written: "He tracked me down the corridors of time. "As it turned out, Earl not only went that night but every night thereafter for six weeks. The only meeting he missed was the women's meeting (they wouldn't let him in!).

After listening to the powerful preaching of Billy Graham for six weeks, at the conclusion of the last service, he found himself standing to his feet, going forward, grabbing Cliff Barrow 's hand, and telling him that God had called him to preach. His next question was, "What do I do now?" Cliff said, "You go to college and prepare," and he recommended his alma mater in South Carolina.

Once again, God had a man prepared to help him take the next step. As the tabernacle cleared out, he saw a man he hadn't seen since grade school. In the beautiful providence of God, this man, Jerry Burleson, was going to the same college in South Carolina that Cliff Barrows had recommended, and he was looking for one more rider. Although it was just two weeks before Fall semester, Jerry assured him that they would accept him on probation though his recommendation. He worked nights for two weeks training another person for his job so that he could leave with the good graces of his employer.

Twelve years and four degrees later (Bob Jones University, B.A., M.R.E.; Dallas Theological Seminary, Th.M., Th.D.), together with broad opportunities of experience in preaching and teaching, overseas missions and military chaplaincy, local church pastor and parachurch ministries, rural and urban outreaches, he ended up not in the pastorate, but in the training of evangelists, pastors, and teachers at Western Seminary. His years there involved traveling over ten million miles and preaching and teaching over twenty thousand hours in over a thousand Bible conferences and thousands of churches.

Among the numerous books and articles that Dr. Radmacher has authored or edited are the following: *You & Your Thoughts* (1977, 2014), *The Nature of the Church* (1978, 1995), *Can We Trust the Bible* (1979), *What to Expect from the Holy Spirit* (1983, 2014), *Hermeneutics, Inerrancy, and the Bible* (1984), *The NIV Reconsidered* (1990), *The Nelson Study Bible* (1997), *Nelson's New Illustrated Bible Commentary* (1999), *Salvation* (2000), and *The Disciplemaker* (2001).

Dr. Radmacher has often stated "In my wildest dreams fifty years ago, I could never have imagined the excited plans that God, in His sovereign grace, had for me." His life mission is found in 2 Timothy 2:15, "Study to show yourself approved unto God, a workman who has no need to be ashamed, rightly dividing the word of truth." His personal life verse is 2 Corinthians 3:18, "But we all, with unveiled face, beholding as in a mirror the glory of the Lord, are being transformed into the same image from glory to glory, just as by the Spirit of the Lord."

www.ingramcontent.com/pod-product-compliance
Lightning Source LLC
Chambersburg PA
CBHW052100070526
44584CB00017B/2265